VENICE REDISCOVERED

VENICE REDISCOVERED

Ronald Shaw-Kennedy

Philadelphia: The Art Alliance Press

South Brunswick and New York

A. S. Barnes and Company

London: Sidgwick & Jackson

Library of Congress Catalog Card Number: 73-22608

A. S. Barnes and Co., Inc.
Cranbury, New Jersey 08512

Associated University Presses, Inc.
Cranbury, New Jersey 08512

Sidgwick & Jackson Ltd
1 Tavistock Chambers
Bloomsbury Way
London, WC1A 2SG

ISBN 0-498-01484-3 (Barnes)
ISBN 0-87982-020-9 (Art Alliance)
ISBN 0-283-98489-9
(Sidgwick & Jackson)

Acknowledgement

The author would like to thank the Superintendent of the Galleries and Works of Art of Venice for his kind help in providing the illustrations.

PRINTED IN UNITED STATES OF AMERICA

Contents

Foreword by The Viscount Norwich

1 Information and Explanations   11

2 History of Venetian Art   20

3 The Piazza San Marco, St Mark's
   and the Doge's Palace   24

4 The Main Churches, Galleries, etc. A–Z   36

5 Summary Notes on Other Churches   115

6 The Grand Canal   117

7 Palaces and Other Buildings not on
   the Grand Canal   123

Index of Artists   124

Foreword

by The Viscount Norwich
Chairman of the Venice In Peril Fund

There is something unfair about Venice. How, one wonders—even when arriving for the fiftieth time—how can the place have quite so much? As the longest-lived republic the world has ever known, the *Serenissima* lasted some eleven hundred years, two centuries longer than English history since the Norman Conquest; for much of that time she was mistress of the Mediterranean, as on more than one occasion her principal rivals—Genoa, Pisa, even Byzantium itself—were forced reluctantly to acknowledge. Her island colonies reached across to the shores of Asia Minor, her merchants were familiar figures from England to Cathay, her diplomatic service was the envy of Europe.

But even that was only the beginning; for Venice was also the loveliest city on earth. And this, more miraculously still, she continues to be—thanks to the sea that surrounds her. That symbolic marriage, annually re-enacted, was no empty ceremony. In her earliest years the sea had been a refuge; later it became a bastion, so effective that not till Napoleon did any would-be invader set foot on the islands of Rialto. Napoleon destroyed the republic; but even he was powerless to change the city which remains, undesecrated by town planner or motor car, still recognizably the Venice of Canaletto and Guardi, and even of Carpaccio.

No city, surely, has been so joyously celebrated by its native painters. (How sadly Florence has fared in comparison!) Yet even they could give no hint of the glories that glowed inside the great churches and palaces they so loved to portray. And that is where Mr. Shaw-Kennedy comes in. His is the first guide-book to Venice I have seen that gives as much attention to the contents of the buildings as it does to the buildings themselves. Henceforth we shall have no more problems in tracking down the works of a favourite painter from one church to another; nor shall we be able to plead inadequate labelling or poor light as an excuse for having missed masterpiece after masterpiece on our morning expeditions.

Such excuses are anyway wearing thinner, since more and more churches are being taken in hand as part of the immense international programme, sponsored by UNESCO, to save Venice from the extinction with which she is now threatened. Mr. Shaw-Kennedy mentions the fact that the Madonna dell'Orto, Tintoretto's parish church and burial-place, was completely restored in 1968-9 through British contributions; and VENICE IN PERIL has since restored Sansovino's Loggetta and San Nicolò dei Mendicoli. We are now at work cleaning and consolidating the Porta della Carta at the Ducal Palace.

on Venice. The old marriage has turned sour and the Adriatic, from being the city's protector, has now become her enemy. St Mark's and its surroundings are sinking 6 cm. every decade, the flooding becomes deeper and more frequent, while atmospheric pollution has accounted for more damage to the stone and marble in the past thirty years than in the previous five centuries. To be sure, the position is not hopeless. Venice *can* be saved. She is the world's responsibility, and the world is coming to her rescue. But time and money are desperately short.

No city of Venice's size has contributed so much to our civilization; and now is the time for us to express our thanks, quickly and as generously as we can. If we do, she will be safe for our grandchildren. If we do not—then this will not only be one of the best of Venetian guide-books; it may also be one of the last.

VENICE REDISCOVERED

1 Information and Explanations

With so many books on Venice, why yet another? This one is written in response to a positive and simple request for a dictionary, as it were, of St Mark's, the Doge's Palace, the Accademia, the churches and other buildings, which will tell you what there is to see in any that you visit without too much detail to sift and without too much discursive talk. It is not therefore intended to supersede any of the other books, either Giulio Lorenzetti's mine of complete information, or those that you can read with pleasure, because of their tales and comments, before you go to Venice or in between your sightseeing excursion while you are there. It is, in short, intended to be truly a guide, convenient to take with you when you are sightseeing, to look into at the church door and to guide you round its walls.

Venice is a beautiful city, with beautiful buildings and beautiful views, wide and handsome or intimate and charming. But it is also full of pictures, some feeble or dull, many good by any standards and some marvellous. They are all over the city, and so hard to discover that even frequent visitors to Venice do not know some of them. Every picture of any merit is to be found here, with brief but adequate comments. There are notes on architecture, with dates to help, but not as much is made of the buildings as of the pictures and the best sculpture that they contain.

When it comes to the pictures and statues and monuments themselves there is some apparent inconsistency. As a rule only those by the great Masters are mentioned. But it is common experience, to which this guide makes concession, that if you are in a small church or a remote one, you want to look at what there is, even if it is not first class, whereas in the large and famous and familiar places you just want to see the best. Thus, for instance, some of the pictures that are mentioned in S. Marziale of S. Zulian would not have scored if they had been in the Frari.

The Index of Artists at the end of the Guide includes pictures and sculptures that are not in the main part, and you will see that in the main part there are notes after some of the narratives referring, by the name of the artist concerned in each case, to those thus omitted. In the Index you will find their subjects and positions. By this means I have tried to cover all that is worthwhile in every narrative, without overcrowding, while leaving it to anyone who is interested in any particular painter or sculptor to seek him out wherever he is represented. The penalty attaching to this method of treating some of the less distinguished artists is the prominence that it gives to that ubiquitous bore, Palma Giovane.

The system by which you are guided round is intended to be the most convenient in each case, and in the churches you usually start at the main door, turning to the right as soon as you have entered it. Aisles are disregarded, and so the right wall of the main part of the church is called the right wall of the nave, whether there are aisles or not, and this wall as a rule comes first. Then the right transept, because transepts branch out on either side of any cruciform church before you come to the part round the high altar. This part is called the chancel throughout and neither apses nor choirs are allowed to confuse the problem of locating a picture or a statue. Apses are usually so much part of the chancel that they can be ignored. Choirs, if they are of no importance, are similarly ignored, but they are mentioned if they are themselves important or contain anything distinctive. They are not always in this part of the church. The Frari's is in the middle of the nave, and in other churches, like S. Sebastiano and S. Alvise, they are above the entrance door.

Each standard itinerary naturally continues and ends with the left transept and the left wall of the nave. In many instances, however, there is a sacristy to visit, or a separate chapel. These ordinarily come in the Guide where their doors are in the church.

There are exceptions to this orderly progress round a church for various reasons, either because the church is so small that you do not need to be led round or because it is so large and there are the grand things to concentrate upon first, as in the Frari, or because you do not enter by the main door, as also in the Frari, or because, as in S. Sebastiano, you should at some stage grasp the whole of the main co-ordinated decorative plan, or simply because in this or that church the formal anti-clockwise circuit just seems wrong. Whatever method seems most convenient has been chosen in each of these cases.

All the churches and other buildings that are worth seeing are in the main part of the Guide. At the end of them there is a list of those that are not worth seeing because they are uninteresting or closed to the public, or both, with a brief note on each of them. After this comes a section on the notable buildings that you can see along the Grand Canal, though any with contents worth seeing (the churches, Cà d'Oro and Cà Rezzonico, for instance) are dealt with fully in the main part. After the Grand Canal there is an index of buildings which are not on it but are of architectural interest.

The alphabetical order presents a problem, because some churches are known by names that are not their full official ones, and here and there it is difficult to decide which you are more likely to look up. S. Zanipolo is a fairly common contraction for SS. Giovanni e Paolo, but not common enough to be preferred. On the other hand the Gesuati and the Gesuiti are names used so generally that many people do not know the full names.

All these three are therefore under 'G'. And you will soon find not only, as this implies, that San, Santa, etc., are ignored as well as 'Church', 'Galleria', 'School', etc., but also that churches and secular buildings are not separated, as they are, maddeningly, in some indexes. Accordingly, except for the Piazza San Marco and the Piazzetta, St Mark's and the Doge's Palace, which are dealt with as special items at the beginning, and the Grand Canal, which comes at the end, you stand a good chance of at once finding what you want if you look for it under the usual name without a prefix, except where the prefix is virtually inseparable, as in Cà d'Oro and Cà Rezzonico.

WHAT TO SEE

The particular difficulty about suggesting a sightseeing programme is that the finest things in Venice are scattered all over it, and so an itinerary for anyone with only a day or two is hard to decide. Moreover, for a picture-lover, the time to get round some large building with a few treasures in it has to be added on to the time it takes to get to it. Or, indeed, there is a straight contrast between the two extremes. The Doge's Palace is, for instance, central but woefully demanding in time and energy in proportion to the number of its good pictures, while the Madonna dell'Orto is, for itself and its contents, the favourite of many who know and love Venice, but so remote that a visit to it takes as long as seeing four or five churches nearer to your starting point. And it is best here to tell the frank truth about getting round. To go by gondola or motor boat is by far the most expensive way, though, as a gondola is quicker than it looks, it is nearly always quickest to use one or the other. If you cannot afford gondolas and want to save your legs, you can use the vaporetto service, including the 'circolare' routes, which go to the Guidecca and on to Cannaregio or the other way round to the north shore. Nevertheless, because there is generally some way to walk to and from the nearest vaporetto station, and because of the huge bends in the Grand Canal, it is usually quicker to walk all the way.*

The best way to guide you for any length of stay seems to be to list the places that must come first, then to put down in detail a programme for four days, and adaptations of it for one day only and for two days, and to leave the rest to you. If you have three or five days, you can adapt the four-day programme. If you have more than this, you can simply choose other places at leisure with the map and the index to it.

---

*The other thing to be said at once is that the churches are usually open until midday, and most of them are open again at four or five o'clock in the evening. You can easily find out opening times for other buildings, some of which vary according to the time of year. Be warned that some (e.g. the Accademia and the Schiavoni) are closed on Mondays.

The picked list is:

1. St Mark's, the Doge's Palace, the Accademia, the Frari and the Scuola di S. Rocco, the Scuola di S. Giorgio degli Schiavoni.
2. S. Sebastiano, SS. Giovanni e Paolo, the Miracoli, the Madonna dell'Orto.
3. The cathedral at Torcello, the Carmini (church and school, listed under Sta. Maria), the group comprising S. Bartolomeo, S. Giovanni Crisostomo, S. Salvatore and Sta. Maria della Fava, S. Stefano.
4. The Salute, S. Giorgio Maggiore, S. Francesco della Vigna, S. Zaccaria, the Fenice Theatre, the Correr Museum.

A fifth list would include the Pietà, S. Giovanni in Bragora, Sta. Maria Mater Domini, S. Trovaso, S. Alvise, S. Silvestro, the Cà Rezzonico, the Gesuiti and [the] Gesuati, but really it might easily include most of the rest in the main part of the guide.

The four-day programme does not accord with this list because it is based partly on geographical considerations. It assumes that you are willing to start out not later than half past nine, seeing that so many churches close at noon, and to start again at about four o'clock and go on until six or when the light fails, according to the time of year.

1st Day	a.m.	Accademia and, if time, either S. Trovaso and the Gesuati or S. Vitale and Sto. Stefano.
	p.m.	S. Rocco (School), the Frari and, if time, S. Giovanni Evangelista or S. Aponal and S. Silvestro.
2nd Day	a.m.	S. Zaccaria, the Schiavoni and S. Giovanni in Bragora.
	p.m.	Sta. Maria Formosa, SS. Giovanni e Paolo, the Miracoli.
3rd Day	a.m.	S. Sebastiano, Carmini (church and school) and, if time, Angelo Raffaelle.
	p.m.	S. Marco and the Doge's Palace and, if time, the Biblioteca Marciana.
4th Day	a.m.	S. Bartolomeo, S. Giovanni Crisostomo, S. Salvatore, Sta. Maria della Fava, the Bovolo.
	p.m.	Madonna dell'Orto and S. Alvise.

If you have only one day, you could see the Frari, the School of S. Rocco and the Accademia in the morning and in the afternoon St Mark's, the Schiavoni, the Colleoni statue outside SS. Giovanni e Paolo and the church itself for a quick look round only, the Miracoli and then, if time is left, S. Maria della Fava or S. Giovanni Crisostomo. It seems quite bold to omit the Doge's Palace, but it can take up too much time when time is precious.

For two days you might use the first two days of the four-day programme, also fitting in St Mark's, and, if you are active, seeing S. Sebastiano on the first morning before the Accademia, leaving out the other churches suggested in the programme for that morning.

Notes: 1. I have included S. Bartolomeo with the other churches for the morning of the fourth day, because it is so close to them, but it is very seldom open. Sunday morning is the best chance.

2. You will be in St Mark's Square and the Piazzetta often enough anyway to look round them. When there you might visit the Museo Correr, which has too many stairs and corridors, but is by St Mark's Square and is open all day.

3. It is worth trying to get into the Fenice Theatre, which is extremely pretty inside. It is not open at regular times, so you can take a chance whenever you are nearby. Very close to it, just beyond the front of the Fenice restaurant and then to the left, is a charming house, now a hotel, with cannons and cannon balls from 1848 all over it.

4. Go one evening to S. Giorgio Maggiore to see the view from its campanile at sunset.

5. A visit to Torcello is a marvellous break. You can do it between twelve noon and four o'clock.

6. Local people, particularly hall porters, are likely to suggest that you go to the Cà Rezzonico and the Cà d'Oro. For true picture-lovers they are not very rewarding, unless you are looking for the 18th century artists represented in the former, and they take up time that could be better spent, unless you are in Venice for a week or two.

HOW TO FIND YOUR WAY

In Venice you can get a detailed, coloured map. I have included a diagram of the city to enable you to place every good church and gallery and to see which are close to one another. I have divided it into the six 'sestieri' and the Guidecca, and have subdivided the larger ones into West and East sectors. Also I have superimposed a small circular area in the centre round the Rialto, for otherwise, this being a meeting point of four sestieri, the churches that are grouped there would have been split up.

INDEX TO MAP

The abbreviated references against the headings in the main text are to this Index.

Rialto
1. S. Giovanni Elemosinario*
2. S. Giacomo di Rialto*
3. S. Giovanni Crisostomo**
4. S. Bartolomeo**
5. S. Salvatore**
6. S.M. della Fava**
7. S. Lio

W. Cannaregio
1. S. Maria dei Penitenti
2. S. Giobe**
3. Gli Scalzi*
4. S. Geremia and P. Labia*
5. S. Alvise**
6. Madonna dell'Orto***
7. S. Marcuola
8. Maddalena
9. S. Fosca
10. S. Marziale
11. Misericordia*
12. S. Felice

E. Cannaregio
1. Gesuiti**
2. Cà d'Oro**
3. S. Sofia
4. SS. Apostoli*
5. S. Canciano
6. S.M. dei Miracoli***

W. Castello
1. S. Lazzaro dei Mendicanti*
2. Scuola di S. Marco*
3. SS. Giovanni e Paolo***
4. Ospedaletto
5. S. Maria del Pianto
6. S. Maria Formosa**
7. Gal. Querini-Stampalia**
8. S. Giovanni Novo
9. S. Zaccaria**
10. S. Giorgio dei Greci
11. La Pietà**
12. S. Francesco della Vigna**
13. S. Giorgio degli
    Schiavoni***
14. S. Giovanni di Malta
15. S. Antonino
16. S. Giovanni in Bragora**
17. S. Martino
18. Arsenale*

E. Castello
1. S. Biagio (and Naval
   Museum)
2. S. Francesco di Paola
3. S. Anna
4. S. Pietro di Castello*
5. S. Giuseppe di Castello
6. S. Elena

S. Croce
1. S. Andrea della Zirada*
2. S. Nicolò da Tolentino*
3. SS. Simeone e Giuda
4. S. Simeone Profeta*
5. S. Giacomo dell'Orio**
6. S. Giovanni Decollato
7. S. Stae* and Gal. d'Arte
   Moderna
8. S. Maria Mater Domini*
9. S. Cassiano*

S. Polo
1. Scuola di S. Giovanni
   Evangelista**
2. S. Rocco*
3. Scuola di S. Rocco***
4. Frari***
5. S. Pantaleone*
6. S. Tomà
7. S. Polo**
8. S. Apollinare*
9. S. Silvestro*

S. Marco
1. S. Benedetto*
2. S. Luca

3. S. Samuele
4. S. Vitale*
5. S. Stefano**
6. S. Maurizio
7. S.M. del Giglio*
8. Fenice Theatre**
9. S. Fantino*
10. Bovolo*
11. S. Gallo
12. S. Moisè*
13. S. Zulian*
14. Capella di S. Basso*
15. Palazzo Patriarcale
16. St Mark's***
17. Doge's Palace***

VAPORETTO STATIONS ☐

1 S. MARCO	5 CA REZZONICO	11 S. STAE
2 SALUTE	6 S. TOMA	12 S. MARCUOLA
3 S. M. DEL GIGLIO	7 S. ANGELO	13 STAZIONE
4 ACCADEMIA	8 S. SILVESTRO	14 PIAZZALE ROMA & 15
	9 RIALTO	
	10 CA D'ORO	

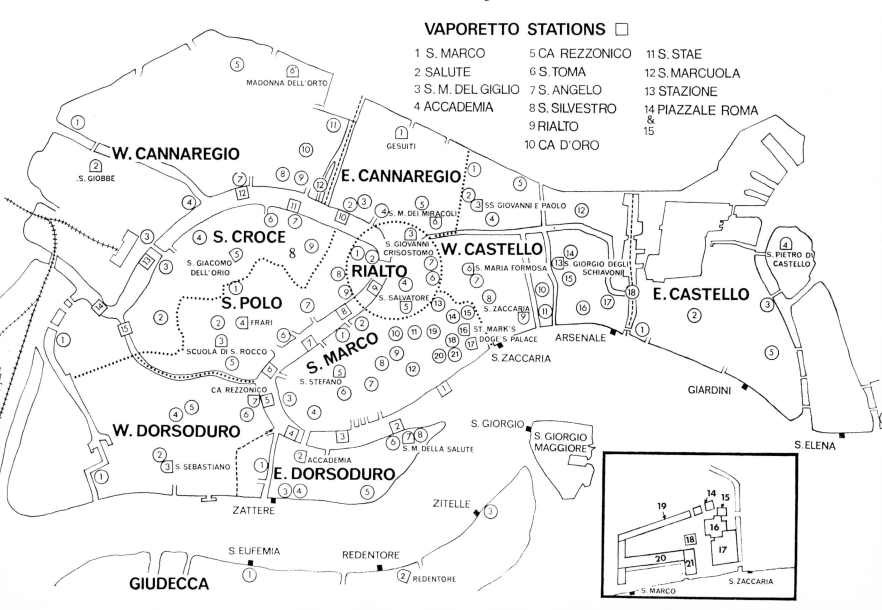

18. Campanile*
19. Procuratie Vecchie*
20. Proc. Nuove and Museo
    Correr**
21. Libreria Sansoviniana*

W. Dorsoduro
1. S. Nicolò dei Mendicoli*
2. Angelo Rafaelle*
3. S. Sebastiano***
4. S.M. del Carmelo***
5. Scuola di S.M. del
   Carmine**
6. S. Barnaba
7. Cà Rezzonico**

E. Dorsoduro
1. S. Trovaso**
2. Accademia***
3. S.M. d. Visitazione
4. Gesuati**
5. Spirito Santo
6. S. Gregorio
7. S.M. della Salute**
8. Pinacoteca Manfrediana*

Guidecca
1. S. Eufemia
2. Redentore**
3. Zitelle

Also***, S. Giorgio Maggiore and the Cathedral at Torcello.

Accordingly, my sectors are Rialto, West and East Canna-regio, West and East Castello, S. Croce, S. Polo, S. Marco, West and East Dorsoduro and the Giudecca. The other islands, S. Giorgio, S. Michele, Murano, Torcello and Burano, naturally are outside these sectors. Inevitably there are some convenient itineraries that cross boundaries. For instance, if you want to reach SS. Giovanni e Paolo from the Rialto you will go through Rialto, S. Marco and West Castello, and the most remote part of S. Polo is conveniently combined with West Dorsoduro. But I believe that most sightseers like to make their own plans and so I hope that with this means of

locating items of interest, and with the suggestions that I have made for a visit of up to four days, you will be able to work things out for yourselves and that you will enjoy this more than following the set walks, often too long or too many, that are to be found in other guides.

Three stars in the map index mean something that you should not miss at any cost. Two stars mean something that you should not miss if time permits. One star means at least one good picture (e.g. S. Silvestro), a beautiful exterior (e.g. S. Apollinare or the School of S. Giovanni Evangelista) or a church or gallery that is likeable or generally worth a visit (e.g. S. Andrea della Zirada or S. Giacomo di Rialto). Of those with no star, three—SS. Simeone e Giuda, S. Anna and S. Biagio—have crept into the map almost by mistake, being not worth a visit but quite likely to be seen on the way here or there. One or two others, like S. Maria dei Penitenti, the Maddalena and S. Giovanni Novo, might be worth a brief visit if they could be found open for once. The rest are all worth seeing if you have time, especially if you can fit them in on the way to something better. You should, for instance, spare a minute or two for S. Marziale on the way to the Misericordia or the Madonna dell'Orto, and for S. Giovanni Decollato when you go to S. Giacomo dell'Orio.

ABOUT THE CITY

This book is designed to help those who want to see the pictures and other treasures of Venice. They may, however, like to know something about the city itself, its past and its future, especially as sometimes pictures or statues refer back to incidents of the past. Moreover, when you are in Venice certain subjects are bound to be talked about.

The city lies in a large lagoon created by the formation of a bar of islands out of silt from three rivers, the Brenta, the Sile, and the Piave. Its real history started with the flight of Italians from the mainland before barbarian invaders, in the 5th and 6th centuries A.D., to the flat mud islands on or within the bar. These were habitable, uninteresting to the invaders, and difficult to attack. Malamocco on the Lido and the island of Torcello were early centres, and then the area which, being beside a deep channel, was called Rivo Alto, contracted later to Rialto. In many places hard clay was found to lie under the mud flats at a depth which allowed buildings to be constructed on piles. Two of the best areas were the site of the Doge's Palace and the large stretch across the main canal which came to be called Dorsoduro because of the size and soundness of its hard clay back. An incalculable number of piles have been used over the centuries, some of oak, some of larch, which are hardened by sea-water. As they could not have been obtained except at great risk in the 5th and 6th centuries when the mainland was still unfriendly, the first settlers must have found enough dry land for their modest huts, but by the 9th century Venice had been consolidated, with an elected Doge, for over a hundred years, and fairly large buildings had already been erected on piles.

When the Roman Empire split into two parts, Venice was nominally a province under Byzantium, but, while trade soon created for her a connection with the eastern Mediterranean, she managed to keep aloof both from Byzantium and from Rome. Soon after A.D. 828, when the relics of St Mark were stolen from Alexandria by Venetians, she had become rich and strong enough to signalize her independence by substituting St Mark for the Greek St Theodore as her patron saint and building a church for him. In the 10th century she declared herself completely independent, and after A.D. 1001, the year in which she asserted her control of the Adriatic, she was recognized as one of the important states of Europe. As it happened, relations between Byzantium and Venice were cordial for most of the next two centuries. All was changed when the Crusaders, transported in Venetian vessels, sacked Constantinople in 1204. From then on power over the territories of the Eastern Empire resided chiefly in Venice herself.

In the years around 1300 the constitution of the city was established. Its effect was that the richest families took over the government, electing from themselves, as the Maggior Consiglio, the Senate and a College of Twenty-Five, and, after 1335, the Council of Ten which held almost all executive authority. The Doge was a figurehead and powerless unless he happened to be a general or an admiral in time of war. Whatever its ideological demerits, the system served Venice well in the 14th and 15th centuries, the period of her enormous increase in power and wealth, her wars, usually successful, with the Turks and the Genoese, and the expansion of her territories on the mainland of Italy, down the eastern Adriatic coast, in Greece and as far as Crete and Cyprus. She became first and foremost a great maritime power, and a custom started that annually on Ascension Day the Doge should go out to the Lido in the state barge *Bucintoro* to celebrate, on reaching open water, the ceremony of the marriage of Venice to the sea. The Arsenal, an enormous dockyard begun in 1155, was repeatedly expanded and strengthened and was virtually completed when its main portal was built in 1460. It is still in use, and Venice is still a busy seaport.

Trade brought foreigners in. The Germans (Tedeschi) had their 'fondaco' or warehouse, and so had even the Turks. By the end of the 12th century many Jews had settled in Venice, giving their name to the island of Giudecca. In 1516, after some vicissitudes, they were moved and confined to the semi-island called Ghetto. Incidentally, the words Arsenal and Ghetto, and also Lido (the last meaning first simply 'seashore' but later a 'seaside resort'), have come into world-wide use from their origins in Venice. During the long period of prosperity Greeks and Dalmatians also settled in Venice and started their 'scuole' or institutes at S. Nicolo dei Greci, alongside the church of S. Giorgio dei Greci, and at S. Giorgio degli Schiavoni (meaning Slavs or Dalmatians) respectively. Other 'scuole' were formed by trades or by religious orders such as the Franciscans' San Rocco, S. Giovanni Evangelista of the Flagellants, and S. Marco of the Dominicans.

The city had grown steadily. First the streams were canalized and some of the paths and open spaces were paved. The name for a street, besides the normal word 'calle', thus became 'salizzada' (meaning paved) or, if it runs alongside a canal or a waterfront, 'fondamenta', meaning an embankment, or 'riva', meaning simply a bank or shore. Later, some canals were filled in, and a street so formed is called a 'rio terra' or 'piscina'. A large square, originally a field, kept the name 'campo', a small one being a 'campiello'.* From the earliest times all sorts of small boats were used on the canals, and the gondola acquired its present shape, or one very close to it, early enough to be recognizable in pictures by Carpaccio. But few now have the little cabins that he portrayed, and it was not until 1562 that a law was passed which made it compulsory for all of them to be painted black. No one knows what the metal prow-head or 'ferro' signifies. A boat-yard in which gondolas are built or repaired

---

*'Ruga', a street lined with shops and dwellings, was never used elsewhere in this sense (which is now obsolete) and means only a 'wrinkle', as it did in Latin. 'Ramo' (branch) is a short connecting street or passage, and 'sottoportico' is a covered way.

is a 'squero', a word used, rarely outside Venice, to mean a covered dock.*

With the canalization of the streams and the reclamation of the mud-banks, plenty of fresh-water springs were found, and Venetian water is extremely wholesome. Some sensible work based on diverting the three rivers that fed the lagoon eventually produced tidal sea-water in all the canals, a natural drainage system which is not perhaps perfect, as your nose will tell you, but is adequate and has freed Venice of malaria.

For a long time there were very few bridged over the canals and the resultant isolation of districts was partly the cause of the division of the population into factions, reduced early on to two covering the whole city, the Castellani in the north-east and the Nicolotti in the south-west. There were serious fights between them for centuries, then tournament competitions when the original point of difference (roughly, the Nicolotti were the old aristocracy and the Castellani were the 'new men') became obsolete. Finally, they arranged a truce, which was to last for ever, when the Austrians came in and were regarded as enemies that both factions wanted to harry. On some bridges you will see footmarks in stone and you may be told that this is where the Nicolotti and the Castellani fought. In fact, the footmarks were the marks for one foot of each of two or four youths who were poised to wrestle on the bridges, but they are all over the city and the wrestling was a sport, not a fight between factions.

The political history of Venice, besides being complicated, is lacking both in notable men and notable events. Doge Enrico Dandolo commanded the Venetians in the Fourth Crusade, and, aged eighty-eight and half blind, led the storming of Constantinople. Doge Marino Falieri was executed for treachery. Two admirals, Vettor Pisani and Carlo Zeno, settled Genoa for good at the siege of Chioggia in 1380. Under Doge Francesco Morosini, late in the 17th century, Venice for the last time fought and beat the Turks. In the wars of the 14th and 15th centuries she employed the overrated and unreliable professional soldiers of fortune called *Condottieri,* as the Pope and other states did. Sir John Hawkwood, whose memorial is in the Duomo at Florence, was English, as were most of his troops, and was one of the earliest and most ferocious of these villains. Later came Braccio da Montone and Attendolo Sforza, contemporaries of Francesco Carmagnola, a general of great ability. After Carmagnola had helped Venice to defeat the Milanese in

*It is derived from the English work 'square', because the tarpaulins used as covers were square.

1427 he was distrusted by the Council of Ten, lured to the city, tortured into confessing treachery and executed. Bartolomeo Colleoni and Erasmo da Narni (Gattamelata) were two others. Colleoni's superb statue is here (see p. 28), and Gattamelata's by Donatello is in Padua.

In 1508 Pope Julius II, anxious to gain a few cities that the papacy had once owned, persuaded France, Spain and Germany, all of whom harboured some jealousy of Venice's prosperity and some indignation over her strength and arrogance, to attack her. The alliance was called the League of Cambrai because there the representatives of the great powers had met and reached agreement. The assailants were partially successful, but by 1517 nearly everyone had changed sides once or twice, and Venice finished with her Italian possessions intact. She was, however, deeply impoverished by her defence, and another blow hit her at the same time. In the early part of the 16th century the Portuguese established their trade route to the East round the Cape of Good Hope, which Vasco da Gama had discovered in 1498. Venice was the principal loser because her wealth depended so much on Eastern trade. To make the situation even worse this was the period in which Turkey, her old rival, became active and strong. The first half of the 16th century therefore saw the beginning of Venice's long decline in power and fortune.

The second half of the city's history is accordingly one of declining power through the 16th, 17th and 18th centuries and then surrender to Napoleon with a token show of resistance in 1797. In 1814 the peacemakers at Vienna, guided by their antipathy to republics, gave Venice to Austria. In 1848 Daniele Manin roused the city to revolt and led the resistance to siege by the Austrians, unsuccessfully in the end but so gallantly that he is revered as a hero. Venice rather reluctantly became part of the new kingdom of Italy in 1866.

The future of the city is mostly concerned with threats to its existence from flooding. In the 18th century the long natural bar, consisting of the Lido and Pellestrina and the Chioggia and Cavallino peninsulas, was reinforced by a stone sea-wall. This was kept up, even by the Austrians, until 1938, since when it has not been repaired. It is composed of huge slabs of Istrian rock, and owing to the neglect of nearly 30 years the storm of 1966 finally broke it. Moreover, the gaps in the sea-wall have been encouraged by the interests that require oil tankers to come through into the new deep channel to Marghera.

At the same time the bed of Venice has sunk, partly because of the enormous amount of fresh water pumped up from beneath it. Also, however desirable the diversion of the three rivers originally was, dams and barrages on other rivers have been erected and so there is no replacement of the seabed by silt. The gradual submersion of Venice may take a very long time, but meanwhile its inhabitants cannot stand repeated flooding of their ground floors, and many have quit the city for Mestre and other nearby places on the mainland. Most of the ancient wooden piles are intact, but it is impossible to calculate how the buildings which rest on them can be raised. Nevertheless a great deal could be done towards preservation if the sea-wall were rebuilt and if the gaps were provided with gates which could be closed when storm and tide produce high water.

The past and the future of Venice having been thus briefly dealt with, it may not be out of place to say a word about the present attractions for a visitor. In each even year there is a large exhibition of modern painting and sculpture in a part of the Giardini Pubblici in which each country has its own pavilion or rooms. This is known as the Biennale. In each odd year there is a special exhibition of some Venetian artist, or of some phase of Venetian art, usually in the Doge's Palace or the Palazzo Grassi. Venice has many good hotels of all grades, and simply walking about the city is a pleasure. Burano still makes lace which nobody much wants, and Murano still makes glass which is on sale in hundreds of shops and good of its kind, although perhaps more attractive in the shop windows than when brought back to an English ambience. Good silk is obtainable, of which the velvet is most likely to have been made in Venice. For those who can afford it, the best of the goldsmiths' work is excellent and cheap for its quality. Lastly let it be said that Venice is a place in which one does not have to seek entertainment. Many visitors enjoy themselves without ever sampling the expensive beaches and restaurants on the Lido. There is, for those who want it, a Casino (in summer on the Lido, in winter in the city itself), and there are often good performances at the Fenice Theatre. But one can be perfectly happy in the evenings in fair weather sitting in the Piazza San Marco, which is undoubtedly the most beautiful and most entertaining square in the world. Three café bands play in it as a rule in the summer, but on some evenings they are replaced by an excellent municipal orchestra.

2 History of Venetian Art

PAINTING

Until the end of the 13th century mosaics were still the main medium of pictorial art, produced first by Byzantines, then by Venetians who had learned from them. In the 14th century and the first half of the 15th painting slowly developed in a primitive style which still reflected its Byzantine origin. Paolo and Lorenzo Veneziano were its best exponents from 1320 to 1380, Stefano di S. Agnese in the 1370s and 1380s, then, more Gothic and less Byzantine, Jacobello del Fiore from 1400 onwards, and finally, from 1420 to 1460, pure Gothic and more powerful than any of his predecessors, Michele Giambono.

In the first half of the 15th century Venice was visited by Gentile da Fabriano and Pisanello, who were followed by Paolo Uccello and Andrea del Castagno, the only one of these four who left there any work that has survived. In Gentile's studio the first native-born Venetian painter was trained. This was Jacopo Bellini (c. 1400 to 1470), who was only a few years younger than Giambono, but was a transitional influence and was blessed with two sons of great talent, Gentile (1429 to 1507) and Giovanni (1430 to 1516), on whom the new ideas of the Renaissance were not wasted. Jacopo seems to have worked in Venice from about 1430 to 1470. Slightly younger was Antonio Vivarini of Murano (c. 1415 to 1476), the founder of his own purely Gothic school, to which belonged Giovanni D'Alemagna (c. 1400 to 1450), Antonio's brother Bartolomeo (c. 1432 to 1499), his son Alvise (1446 to 1504) and Bartolomeo's pupil, Carlo Crivelli (c. 1432 to 1495). Thus these families competed side by side, the Vivarinis with little progress, the Bellinis with giant strides that led to the greatness of Venetian painting.

Giotto painted the Arena Chapel in Padua in the early years of the 14th century, and about 1444 Donatello came there and left his reliefs in the Church of San Antonio, and outside it his statue of the condottiere known as Gattamelata. Andrea Mantegna (1431 to 1506) was born near Padua and was trained there in the arid school of Squarcione. But he was quick to learn from the works of Giotto and Donatello in the city, and with them to guide him, developed into an independent master of great power. He was a contemporary of Gentile and Giovanni Bellini, became their friend and married their sister Nicolosia. Thus, through him and them, there came into Venice the influence of the two outstanding men of genius who had brought art to life in Italy.

Vittore Carpaccio (1455, or 1465,* to 1525) was first a pupil in the school of the Vivarinis, but soon left them to attach himself to Gentile Bellini. He found also in Giovanni Bellini and in Giorgione the influences that affected him most strongly. Cima da Conegliano (c. 1459 to 1517) has been allotted as a pupil to Alvise Vivarini and to Gentile Bellini (also to Montagna, who was only ten years older than Cima), but he formed his style from Antonello da Messina (see below) and Giovanni Bellini. These two were the outstanding younger artists of the generation that was dominated by the Bellinis.

In the next generation the two masters of world importance, Giorgione (1478 to 1510) and Titian (1478, or 1488* to 1576), were Giovanni Bellini's pupils, and Venetian painting reached its zenith with these three men, and through their influence. It is true that Tintoretto (1518 to 1594), whose real name, incidentally, was Jacopo Robusti, was not in Titian's studio long enough to be his pupil, if indeed he was in it at all, but he willingly admitted his influence as well as Michelangelo's. Paolo Veronese (1528 to 1588), whose real name was Paolo Caliari, was another master with genius enough to develop his own independent style, but he also owed a great deal to this main stream of Venetian art and to Titian in particular.

*Carpaccio's and Titian's dates of birth are disputed. I prefer 1465 for Carpaccio, whose first picture in the St Ursula series in the Accademia was painted in 1490 and betrays inexperience. Vasari says that Titian was twenty in 1508, and I can scarcely believe that his last pictures were painted when he was well over ninety.

Here it is right to mention Antonello da Messina (1430 to 1479) (a Sicilian who had probably studied under a Flemish master in Naples), because during a visit to Venice in 1475 he taught the Venetians the use of oil colours. He seems, on the evidence of style, to have had more influence on Cima than any other local painter. But Antonello's importance was that the masterpieces of Giovanni Bellini (for the last forty years of his life), and of Giorgione and Titian and their followers, owed a great deal to the freedom and luminosity that the new medium provided.

Most of the lesser Renaissance painters of Venice were influenced by the Bellinis, directly or at one remove. Giovanni Mansueti (1465 to 1527) was Gentile's pupil. Lazzaro Bastiani (c. 1430 to 1512) was a pupil of Bartolomeo Vivarini, then a close follower of Gentile, and Benedetto Diana (1460 to 1525) was Bastiani's pupil. Both were influenced by Giovanni Bellini, and Diana by Carpaccio. Vincenzo Catena (c. 1470 to 1531) may have been Cima's pupil originally, but was influenced early on by Giovanni Bellini and later by Giorgione. Lorenzo Lotto (1480 to 1556) started as a pupil of Alvise Vivarini, but was to be very much his own master, though with some obligations to Giovanni Bellini and to Giorgione and Titian. Marco Basaiti (c. 1470 to 1435) also started as a pupil of Alvise, but became one of the closest of Giovanni Bellini's followers, with side-glances late in life at Giorgione and perhaps Catena.

Of those who were actually trained in Giovanni Bellini's school most were influenced later by his other pupils. Francesco Bissolo (c. 1465 to 1554), for instance, veered ultimately to Giorgione. Palma Vecchio (1480 to 1528) became very close to Giorgione and to Titian. Rocco Marconi (c. 1480 to c. 1528) seems to have attached himself, after being Giovanni's assistant, to Palma. Andrea Previtali (c. 1475 to 1528) came under Palma's influence and also under Lotto's. Sebastiano del Piombo (1485 to 1547) went through a very marked Giorgionesque period and then left Venice for Rome and Michelangelo.

Bonifazio Pitati (1487 to 1553), usually called Bonifazio Veronese, was a pupil of Palma Vecchio and a follower of Giorgione. Paris Bordone (1500 to 1571) and Andrea Schiavone (1515 to 1563) were Titian's pupils. Jacopo Bassano (1510 to 1592) was a close follower of Bonifazio and influenced by Titian.

Tintoretto and Paolo Veronese bring us close to the end of the 16th century, and then there is a gap which soon becomes an abyss. A few weak followers of the great masters carried on painting dull pictures in the style they had tried to learn. They include Tintoretto's son, Domenico (1560 to 1635), Sante Peranda (1566 to 1638) and Leonardo Corona (1561 to 1605), but the leader and the most prolific painter of this era was Palma Giovane (1544 to 1628), who was Palma Vecchio's great-nephew and in his youth Titian's favourite pupil. After these men there is no artist of any significance until those who revived Venetian painting in the 18th century. The first of these, but by no means the best, was Sebastiano Ricci (1660 to 1734), who had been trained in Milan. Next came Giovanni Battista Piazzetta (1682 to 1754), a chiaroscurist whose style looks back to Caravaggio, but an innovator in tenderness of colour added to a strong mastery of form. The other bright star of the period, Giovanni Battista Tiepolo (1696 to 1770), learnt from Piazzetta, as his early pictures show. His son Giovanni Domenico (1727 to 1804) worked with, and derived from, his father.

In the 18th century also flourished the great *vedutisti,* Antonio Canal, known as Canaletto (1697 to 1768), and Francesco Guardi (1712 to 1793), whose elder brother, Giovanni Antonio (1698 to 1760), was regarded primarily as a figure painter until recent research suggested that several paintings credited to Francesco were by him or by both in collaboration. Bernardo Bellotto (1720 to 1780) was Canaletto's son-in-law and pupil.

Thus ends a succinct account of Venetian painting by Venetian painters. But the Index of Artists at the end of the Guide covers some of the 17th century and 18th century artists whose works are fairly common in Venice but who are not in the main stream, or who followed trends that developed in other parts of Italy. They have only recently attracted interest, and any selection of them has to be somewhat arbitrary. Those chosen for this book are Bernardo Strozzi (1581 to 1644), a Genoese follower of Caravaggio, who painted in Venice and acquired a Venetian love of colour, Francesco Maffei (1625 to 1660), a pupil of Sante Peranda, strongly influenced by Paolo Veronese, Antonio Zanchi (1631 to 1722), Giovanni Antonio Fumiani (1643 to 1710), whose ideal was Paolo Veronese, Nicolo Bambini (1651 to 1736) and Antonio Balestra (1666 to 1740), both Eclectics. Then, truly settecento, Giambattista Pittoni (1687 to 1767), Francesco Zuccarelli (1702 to 1778), a landscape painter who worked in England and was a founder member of the Royal Academy, Pietro Longhi (1702 to 1777), an attractive genre painter, Jacopo Marieschi (1711 to 1794), a follower of Sebastiano Ricci, Jacopo Guarana (1720 to 1808) a prolific pupil of Ricci and Tiepolo, and Pietro Longhi's son Alessandro (1733 to 1813), who specialized in fashionable portraits.

Many of these men were not true Venetians in that they followed Roman or other models. In the Index of Artists there is another category, a small one, that of North Italian artists who painted in Venice or in Venetian style. So there you will find Montagna, Moretto and Savoldo of Brescia, Stefano di Zevio and Negroponte of Padua, and Pordenone and Licinio of Friuli, who do not fit into Venetian history, besides those like Andrea del Castagno and Piero della Francesca, who were complete strangers to Venice but left works there when they were visitors.

ARCHITECTURE AND SCULPTURE

The Venetians made their city rich and powerful in the 9th and 10th centuries and started to embellish it with fine buildings in the 11th. During these three centuries they were bound close to Byzantium by trade and politics and at the same time were cut off from the rest of Italy. Consequently the first artistic influence on their art and architecture was Byzantine. From 1100 onwards this influence was adapted by them to the style we know as Venetian-Byzantine. Arab and Moorish influences came in during this period as well as northern Gothic and Romanesque. None of these ousted the Byzantine origin of Venetian architecture, but all were absorbed into the city's own style. This developed, however, from Venetian-Byzantine to Venetian-Gothic, still a very Benetian blend, in the 14th century. Meanwhile the primitive painters of the 14th century in Venice still looked back to Byzantine mosaics. But from about 1350 onwards sculpture started to break from tradition through two families of stonemasons, the De Sanctis family first, then the Delle Masegne, who both produced works that displayed originality and a new vigour in contrast with the decadence of the old tradition.

In the 15th century an architectural influence from the mainland of Italy, which had barely been felt in the second half of the previous century, began to affect the basic design of churches built in this period in Venice. Sculpture and the decoration of buildings remained essentially Venetian-Gothic through the domination of Giovanni Bon and his son Bartolomeo, but the Tuscan Renaissance had begun to infiltrate with sculptors like Nicolo Lamberti, his son Pietro, and his pupils. It was thus a period of transition, and culminated, about the middle of the century, in the Venetian-Renaissance style, of which the brothers Antonio and Paolo Bregno were the first great masters. Lombards by origin, and alert to the progress of the Renaissance in Tuscany, they worked, Antonio at sculpture, Paolo at architecture, simultaneously with Giovanni Bon for many years, and blended his development of Venetian-Gothic into Venetian-Renaissance instead of renouncing it.

So too did other Lombard immigrants, the most famous of whom, Pietro Solari and his two sons Antonio and Tullio, worked in Venice from 1468 to 1532 and were known as the Lombardi. The church of the Miracoli is their masterpiece. Contemporary with them were Mauro Coducci, from Bergamo, and Antonio Rizzo, from Verona, two outstanding architects (Rizzo was an outstanding sculptor also) who at this time moved further away from the decorative Venetian style than did the Lombardi, and nearer the classical teaching of the mainland.

The other early Venetian-Renaissance architects whose work is still to be seen in the city are Antonio Gambello (1430 to 1481), Giorgio Spavento (1440 to 1509), Antonio Abbondi, known as Lo Scarpagnino (1475 to 1549), Guglielmo dei Grigi (1470 to 1530), and Bartolomeo Bon of Bergamo (1445 to 1529), a pupil of Coducci.

It was in 1481 that Verrocchio came to Venice and modelled the famous equestrian statue of Bartolomeo Colleoni which stands outside SS. Giovanni e Paolo. This statue was cast and finished and its pedestal was designed by Alessandro Leopardi, who became the leading sculptor in Venice and remained so until his death in 1523.

A new phase of architecture in the city opened with the arrival of Michele Sanmicheli from Verona in about 1520. He was primarily a military architect, but designed civil buildings also, and his Palazzo Grimani on the Grand Canal is the earliest purely classical building in Venice. He was followed in 1527 by Jacopo Tatti, known as Sansovino, a Florentine who worked in Rome before its sack in that year. Sansovino remained in Venice until his death in 1570, and filled it with his works, which were in the style he had learned on the mainland, though he made a slight concession to local tradition by incorporating more decoration than Roman and Florentine canons permitted. And in 1560 came Andrea Palladio, already famous for his work in Vicenza. He made no concession to local tradition, criticized the Ducal Palace, designed S. Giorgio Maggiore, the Redentore and the facade of S. Francesco della Vigna, and left without inspiring a single follower. The succeeding generation, of whom Vincenzo Scamozzi was pre-eminent in architecture, and Alessandro Vittoria in sculpture, preferred to follow in the wake of Sansovino.*

The next stage in Venetian architecture was the spread of late Renaissance baroque from the mainland, with which cultural connections were now as close as once they had been remote. The period is that covered by the end of the 16th and all of the 17th century. Baldassare Longhena, the principal baroque architect of Venice, was born there in 1598 and died in 1682, having designed his most notable work, the church of the Salute, in time to see its construction started two years before his death. Guiseppe Sardi (c. 1630 to 1699), who is well represented in the city, came there first in 1665. In sculpture Vittoria, who was still the leader until he died in 1608, tried to combine the styles of Michelangelo and Sansovino. Younger by twenty-five years, and rather more influenced by the new tendencies, was Girolamo Campagna, who worked in Venice at least until 1626 and was by far the most distinguished sculptor of his generation. Also two sculptors from Genoa, essentially baroque, Nicolo Roccatagliata and his son Sebastiano, were in Venice at intervals in the early part of the 17th century and left some work of charming quality. After them sculpture was represented, as was architecture, by feebler practitioners, many deriving their ideas from Bernini, who led the whole of Italy for most of the 17th century. Last of all, and much later, Antonio Canova started in Venice, came back to work there from time to time, and died there in 1822.

*Scamozzi was for a time a pupil of Palladio, and may have worked with him on San Giorgio (see p. 103) but later he went his own way.

3 The Piazza San Marco, St Mark's and the Doge's Palace

The references against each heading are to the map index

The Piazza San Marco and the Piazzetta
SM 18, 19, 20, and 21

At the east end of the Piazza is St Mark's. Its west end was reconstructed by Napoleon, and the present building that fills it is his. On the north side are the old Procuratie (residence of the Procurators or chief administrative officers of the city), early 16th century, built by Mauro Coducci, his pupil B. Bon, Guglielmo dei Grigi and Sansovino, and the Clock-Tower, the central part of which was designed by Mauro Coducci. It was completed just before 1500 together with the bell and the bronze figures that strike it, but the side pieces of the tower were added some years later. On the south is the new Procuratie, a building which was begun by Vincenzo Scamozzi in 1582 and carried on by Longhena, who finished it in 1640. Scamozzi's part starts at the corner of the Piazzetta, and where it ends, just after the tenth window from that corner, the style of the windows changes slightly.

The Campanile is a faithful replica of the original, which was finally completed early in the 16th century and fell in 1902. The figures of Venice and of Justice high up on the east and west side respectively, above the belfry canopy, were put together from the fragments of the original figures after the fall, as also was the gilded figure of the Archangel Gabriel on the summit. The largest bell, the Marangona, was the only one that survived the fall.

At the foot of the Campanile facing the entrance to the Doge's Palace is Sansovino's beautiful little Loggetta. It was damaged when the tower fell, but not too badly. The statues on the front, by Sansovino himself, are of Athene, Apollo, Hermes and Eirene. The balustrade and its elegant gate are early 18th century additions by Antonio Gai.

The bases of the three flagpoles in front of St Mark's date from the first years of the 16th century and were designed by Leopardi. On the southernmost pole is Neptune receiving from a Satyr the Fruits of the Earth in the form of grapes. On the centre pole is a mixed allegorical scene showing Justice (as often, a symbol for Venice) with an elephant (strength and justice) below, and Pallas Athene with dolphins and seahorses. The northern pole has Tritons and Nereids carrying the fruits of the sea.

The Piazzetta, which leads off the Piazza and is overlooked by the Doge's Palace, is officially the Piazzetta San Marco but is always called simply the Piazzetta, there being only one other in Venice, the Piazzetta dei Leoncini on the north side of St Mark's. On its south side, against the open water, stand two pillars, with the Lion of St Mark on the left-hand one and St Theodore, the earlier patron saint of Venice, on the right hand. Both look landwards. The lion is an ancient mythological animal, Etruscan, Persian or even Chinese, which had its wings added in Venice to make it into a Marcian lion. St Theodore is a copy of a composite statue made up of Roman and early Italian parts and now somewhere in the Ducal Palace.

On the west side of the Piazzetta is the building usually called the Libreria Sansoviniana, which contains also the library known as the Biblioteca Marciana. The Biblioteca is in fact in the old mint (Zecca), which adjoins the Libreria on the Molo. Its entrance, by Scamozzi, with giant figures at the sides by Campagna and Aspetti, is however in the Libreria arcade, six arches nearer the Molo than the Libreria's own portico, which bears two large caryatids by Vittoria and his pupils. The Libreria is a masterpiece designed by Sansovino, started by him in 1540 and finished in 1588 after his death. With its line he created the Piazzetta as a broad second axis, at right angles to that of the Piazza, thus completing his great plan for this superb site, which he had been asked to lay out and beautify. With shops in their arcades, café tables in front of them and no free ends to give them visible shape, the Libreria and the two Procuratie in the Piazza tend to be taken for granted. If the Libreria itself were a separate building and not part of so familiar a group, it would be more striking and perhaps more admired.

Inside it, on the ceiling of the vestibule at the top of the marble staircase, is a late picture by Titian of 'Wisdom'. Ruskin called it 'a most interesting work in the brilliancy of its colour and its resemblance to Veronese'. In the main room there is a good collection of books, some illuminated, and a number of formal pictures. Of the allegorical figures on the ceiling a row of three, the sixth row from the door, Song, Music and Honour, by Veronese, are easily the best. His also are the figures of philosophers on either side of the door. Of the other philosophers ranged round the walls all those on the left wall, except the first two, are by Tintoretto, as also is the one next to them on the wall that faces the door. The first two on the left, as well as the end row of three on the ceiling, are by Andrea Schiavone, who comes off better on a smaller scale.

(Also in Index of Artists: B. Bon of Bergamo, Spavento)

St Mark's (Plate 1)   SM 16

The basic architecture of this splendid church, which is known as the 'Basilica di San Marco' (although not architecturally a basilica) is pure Byzantine, but its decoration is Venetian-Byzantine. It was built in the 11th century, and the main structure was complete by 1100 but unadorned: During the centuries following the facade, the arcade, the entrance and the interior were repeatedly enriched with mosaic and marble and carved stone. The white edges of the upper arches, which were gilded at first, are part of the decoration of 14th-15th c. as are the twelve figures of saints on their summits (they continue on the north and south sides) and the thirteen lanterns, with figures in them, that occupy the gaps between them. The rail of the gallery over the lower arches is 13th century, and the six bas-reliefs between it and them, though some are much older, were placed here at this time.

Of the original mosaics that were made for the facade, also in the 13th century, only the lunette under the left arch and the black and gold decorations just above the other doors survive, the lunettes that are now in the other arches being 18th century (next left), 19th (central) and 17th (both on right, and the four above), all quite unsuitable. But it would be possible to replace them with copies of the original mosaics, which are clearly reproduced in a picture by Gentile Bellini in the Accademia. The four horses were brought from Byzantium in 1204 (they had been made in Rome for a triumphas quadriga in Nero's time and taken to Byzantium by Constantine), and in the 14th century were placed where they now stand. The central window was originally completed with an open stonework screen, but old prints show that it was not very handsome. The facade is so great that it gets away with the present black vacuum in this main window as well as with the dreadful mosaics. On the summit of the arch round the window the statue of 'St Mark' is by Nicolo Lamberti, and so are the angels on either side. The 'Evangelists', the 'Madonna' and the 'Angel of the Annunciation' below are by his son Pietro. They or their pupils did much of the rest of the carving on this and the other arches.

Small items of some interest on the facade are, at the right edge, the Pietra del Bando, a block of porphyry from which edicts were read, and which incidentally took the force of the crumbled masonry when the Campanile fell in 1902, the crude early carvings over the central door, and, one at each end, below the main parapet on the small balconies that interrupt the pillars, not easy to spot, two little grotesque figures carrying jugs, about which (where they came from, why they are there) nobody knows anything at all. Round the corner on the north wall is a very fine Gothic doorway. In the little square here, the Piazzetta dei Leoncini, are the two lions which give the Piazzetta its name and have acquired fame principally because children are not forbidden to climb over them. The Palazzo Patriarcale is at the east end.

In the vestibule are very good 13th century mosaics, especially those on the ceiling, including, in the main atrium, as you go in, scenes from Genesis. In front of the main doorway are three red marble slabs with a small diamond-shaped decoration in the centre one, to mark the place, so they say, where Frederick Barbarossa abased himself before the Pope in 1177. The door on the right is the Porta di San Clemente, 13th century Venetian-Byzantine, inlaid with silver and once enamelled.

Inside, St Mark's is very dark and cool, and, in a rather stern way, most impressive. It once had more windows and more light, but now it is often hard to see much of the decoration. The walls are covered with panels of rare stone, not, to be sure, very bright or very clean, and with mosaics, mostly of the 14th century, but some earlier and some later, variously depicting Christ and his saints. Some of the finest are that of 'Christ between the Virgin Mary and St Mark', over the entrance door, that on the right wall of the nave of

2A   St Mark's. Mosaic in cupola over chancel

'The Agony in the Garden', and those in the central cupola of the 'Ascension' and, on the arch to the west of it, of the 'Crucifixion' and the 'Resurrection'. All these, besides those in the other cupolas and the apse above the chancel, are 12th or 13th century. So are the purely decorative borders and intervals, which are in their way as good as most of the scenes.

In front of the chancel is the Iconostasis, a screen surmounted by a curious bronze and silver crucifix between imposing 14th century Venetian-Byzantine figures of the Virgin, St Mark and the Apostles by the Delle Masegne brothers. Through it you can see, but not very well, bas-reliefs by Sansovino on the sides of the two small tribunes to right and left. All that is beyond you can see by paying for admission to the Pala d'Oro (see below). First come two short altar rails with four bronze figures on each, the four central ones (that is the two on each rail nearest the gap between them) of the Evangelists being also by Sansovino. The carved marble pillars which form a sort of baldacchino are thought by some to be 13th century Venetian, by others 5th or 6th century from Byzantium. Above are six marble statues, Christ between St Mark and St John in front and "The Redeemer" between St Matthew and St Luke behind. All are 13th century except the figure of Christ, which is an 18th century replacement. Against each of the side walls are three statues on brackets, German work, in company too good for them.

On the back of the High Altar is the Pala d'Oro, a magnificent altarpiece, gold and silver encrusted with jewels and decorated with enamel. Most of it is Byzantine, as it was originally commissioned from Constantinople in the 10th century and added to with panels also made there about 1100. Later it was remade in Venice, with a few additions, in 1345. The bronze sacristy door, which is behind the altar, is a great work by Sansovino. On it are two beautiful bas-reliefs of the 'Descent from the Cross' and the 'Resurrection' and on the surround are six heads, purporting to be of Prophets or of Fathers of the Church, but actually portraits of Paolo Veronese (top right), Titian (top left), Sansovino himself (below Veronese), Pietro Aretino (below Titian) and Palladio, one of the two unidentified at the bottom. The little gilded door on the altar in the centre of the wall facing the Pala d'Oro is again by Sansovino, and the figures of 'St Francis' and 'St Bernardino' on either side of it are by Lorenzo Bregno.

In the Baptistery, entered from the right of the nave, there is a fine Renaissance font, probably the work of two or three sculptors, and there are mosaics of the 14th century depicting the childhood of Christ in the right-hand room, the life of John the Baptist in the others and, on the left wall, the Crucifixion. They illustrate their transitional period by the conventional Byzantine style of the 'Baptism of Christ' alongside the northern Gothic influence in the 'Adoration of the Magi' and the Italian influence in the 'Dance of Salome'. On the far wall is a mural tomb of Doge Andrea Dandolo, who commissioned the mosaics and died in 1354. By the De Sanctis, it is sincere and grand and historically important. The Zen chapel, which leads off the Baptistery (and has another door leading from the vestibule), contains a beautiful bronze statue of the 'Virgin and Child' by Antonio Lombardo, by whom also are the reliefs of 'God the Father' and 'Angels with Musical Instruments' in the canopy above it.

To run now rather rapidly round all the rest, along the right wall of the nave, first comes a triple Byzantine bas-relief of 'The Redeemer between the Virgin Mary and St John the Baptist' and the Baptistery door. Beyond, on one of the thick square pillars, is a 12th century bas-relief of the 'Madonna and Child' worn away by kisses. Round into the right transept we face the 13th century Treasury door, which is of Moorish design. High above in the end wall is a 14th century rose window. On and round to the east side of this transept the only altar is of hagiological but not artistic interest. Between it and the chancel lies the chapel of S. Clemente (through which you pass to the Pala d'Oro, etc.) with 12th century mosaics that are much admired. Over its entrance are figures probably by the Delle Masegne of the 'Virgin and Child' between St Christina, St Clare, St Catherine and St Agnes. Between the entrance and the chancel, the 14th century Gothic wall-piece is perhaps also by the Delle Masegne. The pair to it is in the corresponding place on the left of the chancel, and in front of the chancel-chapel on that side, which is St Peter's, is the pair to the architrave over the entrance to the S. Clemente chapel, with the 'Virgin and Child' again in the centre and on either side St Mary Magdalene, St Cecilia, St Helena and St Margaret, in the style at least of the Delle Masegne.

We have now passed the two pulpits, each put together from ancient materials. On square pillars near by, facing down the nave, are two figures, St James on the right, 15th century, and St Paul with the Sword of the Spirit on the left,

2B   St Mark's. Sacristy door, the 'Resurrection' by Sansovino

a 16th century figure on a 15th century altar. On the innermost side of the same pillar is a Byzantine icon, the 'Madonna of Consolation'. In the left transept, on the altar on the east side, there is a small Byzantine painting called the 'Madonna Nicopeia' encrusted with jewels but more interesting for the veneration in which it is held than for any great artistic value. At the end, in the chapel of St Isidore you will see an imposing 14th century sarcophagus on which lies the figure of the Saint, an angel above him, and outside the arch 'The Madonna' and the 'Angel of the Annunciation'.

Next to this chapel is that called 'della Madonna dei Mascoli', its early 15th century altar mostly by Bartolomeo Bon, and late mosaics, those on the left designed by Giambono and those on the right designed perhaps by Mantegna. Back into the nave, on the inward side of a square pillar at the corner of this transept, is the 'Madonna dello Schioppo', a 13th century bas-relief with a 19th century rifle fixed alongside it as a votive offering.

The Treasury contains various rare objects, many of great value, and some quite beautiful or interesting. It consists of three rooms, the Ante-Treasury, which you enter first, the Sanctuary through to the left, and the main part, the Treasury itself, to the right. In the Sanctuary, high up on the wall facing you as you enter is a 6th century Byzantine marble bas-relief of 'Christ and the Apostles' with 'Christ and two Angels' above it, probably parts of the same sarcophagus. As you go from the Ante-Treasury into the Treasury itself, on the left is the stone seat known as 'St Mark's Throne'. It is 6th or 7th century Alexandrine and was given by the Byzantine Emperor to the Patriarch of Grado. In the treasury on the entrance wall, to the left as you enter, are four fine Byzantine icons. Against the left wall, besides two 15th century silver-gilt candlesticks and two altarpieces (that below 13th century but mutilated, that above early 15th century) are, high up on green marble columns, a 'Madonna' and 'Angel of the Annunciation' of about 1400, which show the first Florentine influence on Venetian sculpture. The vitrines contain chalices and other objects, mostly labelled, including a fine simple crystal bowl in the first vitrine on the left.

The Museo Marciano is also worth a visit because it has a great series of early 15th century tapestries of the life of Christ and a fine polyptych by Paolo Veneziano and his sons, and because it gives you close views of some of the mosaics and of the bronze horses. It used to have the organ doors by Gentile Bellini which are now in the Capella di San Basso.

(Also in Index of Artists: Paolo Veneziano, Ricci, and, for the Palazzo Patriarcale, Bambini and Guarana.)

The Doge's Palace   SM 17

The Palace has St Mark's attached to it on the north, and on the east is a fairly narrow canal crossed by the Bridge of Sighs and by the Ponte di Paglia at the point where it emerges through the Molo (i.e. the quay) into open water. On the other side of this canal are the prisons to which the Bridge of Sighs leads, thus earning its name. On this side, beyond the first thirty feet, the Palace walls are, like the bridge, of early Renaissance architecture, and so is the courtyard, which is largely the work of Sansovino.

The south side of the Palace, looking over the Molo and the wide expanse of the Bacino, and the west side, on the open Piazzetta, are its most visible aspects, and, in accordance with the tendency of all things in Venice to appear to go right by chance, these walls are the perfectly beautiful Venetian Gothic walls of the 14th century, when the Palace was first rebuilt in its present form. It is true that the south-east corner was destroyed by fire in the 16th century, but it was then rebuilt so as to be now indistinguishable from the rest.

The design is unique, and defies, I believe, certain principles of traditional architecture, but is still completely successful. At ground level are large, low, simple Gothic arches, above them narrow and more elaborate ones, and, above them again, the main walls, faced with a pattern of marble, apricot and white and dark grey, which has never been surpassed as a surface for a building of this size in all degrees of light. The windows are perfect in design and proportion. Those on the Molo side are neither uniform nor in line, but their pattern is entirely satisfactory. On top of the walls the traceried white stone coping (with graceful little pagodas at the corners) is a light and delicate final embellishment that completes the impression that the Palace gives of having been made without the guidance of any theory by hands that could not make anything wrong and could not make anything ordinary.

Over each of the two main central windows, one on the Molo side and the other on the Piazzetta side, is a statue of 'Justice' by Alessandro Vittoria. The capitals on the columns are all different, and at the corners are fine, bold, unsophisti-

3　The Doge's Palace

cated representations of biblical subjects, the 'Drunkenness of Noah' by the Ponte della Paglia, 'Adam and Eve' at the junction of the Molo and the Piazzetta, both by the same Lombard hand, and (a little later, less ingenuous and decidedly Tuscan) the skilful 'Judgement of Solomon' at the corner nearest St Mark's. Above these are Gothic figures of the Archangels Raphael, Michael and Gabriel respectively (all either by Bartolomeo Bon or Antonio Bregno), and in one of the 'eyes' between them a bas-relief of 'Venice as Justice'. The main door, called the Porta della Carta, the work of

Giovanni and Bartolomeo Bon, forms with its surround a magnificent elaborate Gothic façade. The Doge and Lion are 19th century reproductions. 'Temperance' and 'Fortitude' in the lower niches are by Pietro Lamberti, and 'Prudence' and 'Charity' above are probably by Antonio Bregno.

The porphyry group low down on the left before you get to the door, and in fact on the corner of the Treasury of St Mark's, was one of the spoils brought from Byzantium. It is called the 'Four Moors' (but also the 'Tetrarchs'). Spoils also from early wars are the other decorations, reliefs and

31

columns and so on, on the wall between the 'Four Moors' and the gateway and along the adjacent wall of St Mark's. The small mosaic Madonna high up on this wall is lit at night, originally in pursuance of a vow made by a sailor who miraculously survived a storm, now by custom.

One gruesome reminder of the execution of early Venetian justice is on the side of the Palace facing the Piazzetta. There is, in the upper row of arches, one which is darker than the rest, with a reddish tinge. It was here that those who had offended against the State and had been condemned to death were publicly strangled and left hanging as a warning to others.

In the courtyard you will see that there is a mixture of architecture but that most is Renaissance. The date of it is around 1500, and the whole of the main building on the east side was reconstructed, after a serious fire in 1483, by Rizzo, Pietro Lombardo, Spavento and Scarpagnino, and finally Sansovino. The principal external staircase, called the 'Giants' Staircase', by Rizzo, has at its summit two statues by Sansovino of 'Mars' and 'Neptune'. Leading to it from the Porta della Carta is the Arco Foscari, started by the Bon family in 1443 in the Gothic style, but taken over in 1450 by Bregno, who grafted Renaissance architecture on to it and, with Rizzo, decked it with Renaissance statues.

The internal staircase is the Scala d'Oro, steep and long and highly decorated in stucco by Vittoria. The prescribed tour is of rooms on the second and third floor (third and fourth in American parlance), and, as you start it on the third, there are 130 steps of the Scala d'Oro to climb first. Also there is a very long walk ahead before you can get out. For these reasons, and because there are many second-rate pictures, it is wise to concentrate on the best.

Somewhere, and I mention it first because, though it is often moved, it recently was on an easel on a landing passed through on the ascent, is one of Tiepolo's best pictures, 'Neptune offering the Riches of the Sea to Venice'. It is less logical to mention here also two fine statues of 'Adam' and 'Eve' by Rizzo, because recently they were right at the very end of the prescribed route round the Palace.* They were, however, placed elsewhere, nearer the start of the route, not long ago and may be moved again. They are the originals, in marble, and the copies in the courtyard will show you where they used to stand facing the Giants' Staircase.

Back to the third floor, in the square room at the top of the stairs (Salotto Quadrato) the picture in the centre of the ceiling is by Tintoretto and represents 'The Virgin and St Jerome attending the Presentation by Justice of Sword and Scales to Doge Priuli'. The next room (Sala delle Quattro Porte), a rectangular one that spans the building, has a truly dreadful stucco ceiling, the pictures in which were by Tintoretto but are so damaged and restored and repainted as to be valueless. On the entrance wall a huge set-piece, started by Titian and finished by his son, represents 'Doge Grimani kneeling to Faith, and St Mark', with a circus lion and with figures at the sides that Titian never had a hand in. On the wall on the right, and so farthest from the entrance, is a copy of Tiepolo's easel picture mentioned above in the position where the original should be.

In the next room, which is square (the Ante-Collegio), are the best pictures of all, four by Tintoretto and one, of 'Europa', by Veronese. The subjects of those by Tintoretto are the 'Forge of Vulcan', 'Mercury and the Graces', 'Minerva repelling Mars from Peace and Prosperity', and, most beautiful of all, 'Bacchus and Ariadne' with Venus holding a starry coronet over Ariadne's head. The 'Return of Jacob' is by Jacopo Bassano, and the spoiled centre picture in the ceiling is by Veronese.

Next is an oblong room (the Collegio) in which all the ceiling pictures are good ones by Veronese*. At the far end is an equally good picture by him of 'Thanksgiving for Victory in the Battle of Lepanto', between grisailles (also by him) of 'St Sebastian' and 'St Justina'. The other pictures are by Tintoretto and his assistants. The large one on the entrance wall, of 'Doge Gritti presented to the Virgin Enthroned, with Three Saints', is mostly school work. The three on the wall facing the window are, from right to left, the 'Mystical Marriage of St Catherine, with Doge Donato', 'Doge da Ponte worshipping the Virgin', and 'Doge Mocenigo being presented to Christ by St Mark'. Assistants must have contributed to them, probably most to 'Doge da Ponte' and least, if at all, to 'Doge Donato'.

Now you move to the right into a huge room (the Senato) which has no good pictures but a fine ceiling. The last picture on the left on the entrance wall, of 'St Mark and two other Saints presenting Doge Loredano to the Virgin', is given to Tintoretto himself by Berenson, but by others largely to

*Unhappily the prescribed route is sometimes changed, but the rooms are named. By one alternative route you go through the 'Stanze Private' (see later) on the way up, and you may find Tiepolo's picture there. You may even start on the second floor.

*The subjects are all qualities or allegories appropriate to Venice; down the centre 'Strength' (Mars and Neptune), 'Faith' and 'Victory'; along the left side 'Honour', 'Innocence', 'Humility' and 'Trust'; along the right side 'Peace', 'Logic', 'Vigilance' and 'Wealth'.

The Doge's Palace
'Bacchus and Ariadne'

assistants or entirely to his son Domenico. There is nothing worth seeing in the two rooms (Chiesetta and Ante-Chiesetta) that are entered by the door at the end of the left, past the dais, except in the former, over the altar, a group of the 'Virgin and Angels' by Sansovino. Back through the Senato and the 'Quattro Porte' and a passage you come to a large room (Sala Consiglio dei Dieci) with ceiling paintings of which two are by Veronese, one of a turbaned man and a girl, in the far right-hand corner as you stand with your back to the window, and the long one on the left, of 'Juno dropping Crowns, Wreaths, a Jewel and Gold Coins on to Venice'. In the next room (Sala della Bussola) a small cupboard let into the panelling is connected with a slot in the wall of the landing beyond, once covered by a lion's mask, this being the famous 'Bocca di Leone' into which secret, though not anonymous, denunciations were placed. The marble fire-

places in this and the next room were designed by Sansovino.

You then pass into the Sala dei Capi, and the ceiling picture nearest the entrance door, the 'Punishment of a Forger', is by Veronese. So is the one diagonally opposite it, of 'Victory and Sin', but it has been badly damaged and badly restored. In the next room, that of the Inquisitors, the 'Return of the Prodigal' and the other pictures on the ceiling, figures of 'Virtues', are ascribed by some to Tintoretto, though not by Berenson. In the four armoury rooms which follow are three bronze busts by Aspetti, of Agostino Barbaro, Doge Sebastiano Venier and Marcantonio Bragadin. As you come back and out down a few stairs, opposite you over a door is a marble bust of Venier again, this time by Vittoria. And, through this door, in the far wall is the slot (see above) of the Bocca di Leone.

On the second floor, to which you now descend, the first room, the Sala Scarlatti, has a fine fireplace by the Lombardi, and an elaborate ceiling. The next, the Sala dello Scudo, and two that follow are of no interest. Then there is a long narrow room called the Sala dei Filosofi, which you cross as you turn right out of the last of the dull rooms in the courtyard side.* Out of it leads a small staircase. Walk up it, turn round and there over the entrance is Titian's fresco of 'St Christopher', somewhat retouched but well worth seeking out. Tiepolo's 'Neptune offering the Riches of the Sea to Venice', mentioned above, may be one of the group in the Stanze Private del Doge, which you next enter. And in them or near by are to be found a dark, tragic 'Pietà' by Giovanni Bellini, a splendid 'Lion of St Mark' by Carpaccio, four strange works by Hieronymus Bosch, an 'Entombment' ascribed to Antonello da Messina and the 'Mocking of Christ' by Quentin Matsys.

From here on there is no picture worth seeing until at last

you reach the huge Sala del Maggior Consiglio. Here is the largest serious picture in the world, Tintoretto's 'Paradiso', painted in its most important features by him and, where he had to use his son Domenico, his pupil Palma Giovane and his studio men, so carefully supervised that it is a complete work of art due solely to his skill and authority. Ruskin once called it the largest and therefore the best picture in the world. Though he did not always give it quite so much praise, and though other distinguished art critics suggest that it is so ambitious that it cannot be completely successful, it is right to look at it as a picture with great merits that transcend the mere fame of its enormous size.

Elsewhere in this hall are many other pictures, none of first-class importance except two by Veronese, one, the large oval in the ceiling nearer the 'Paradiso', of 'The Apotheosis of Venice', and the other, a late work, between the windows on the end wall opposite the 'Paradiso', of 'Doge Andrea Contarini returning in triumph from the Battle of Chioggia'.* The portraits on the frieze are of the Doges. In the remaining large room (Sala dello Scrutinio) there is a grand picture by Tintoretto of the 'Battle of Zara' (extreme right on the courtyard side), but otherwise there is nothing else in the Palace to delay an exhausted sightseer, except a tour of the prisons.

(Also in Index of Artists: Bambini, Jacobello del Fiore, Palma Giovane, Peranda, Ricci, Domenico Tiepolo, Domenico Tintoretto, Aspetti, Bregno of Como, Campagna, Delle Masegne, Palladio, Vittoria. But some of their references are to the Sala Gattamelata, Sala dello Scrigno and the Avogaria, which includes the S. dei Notai and S. dei Censori, and these rooms, on the first floor, are not in the prescribed tour.)

*Unless, depending on which route is being used, you walk down this room after passing through the Sala Scarlatti and Sala dello Scudo.

*Berenson does not ascribe this to Veronese, and it looks as if it were mostly (or all) school work, like the first two on the ceiling on either side of the 'Apotheosis'.

5
The Doge's Palace
'Europa' by Paolo Veronese

4 The Main Churches, Galleries, etc. A–Z

The Accademia ED 2

Shut on Mondays, open 10 a.m.–1 p.m. on Sundays and some holidays. On other days hours are 10 a.m.–2 p.m., and the attendants start to clear the gallery well before closing time, so it is best to go in the morning. The building is a reconstruction of an old group that consisted of a church, Sta. Maria della Carità, a monastery and a church school.

Room I

This is full of Venetian primitives, the less good of them being not worth lingering over with so many marvellous things ahead. Paolo Veneziano, the doyen of the Venetian primitives (he worked in the first half of the 14th century) is best represented by the 'Coronation of the Virgin' in his altar-piece that faces you as you enter the room. There is also a 'Madonna' by him on the reverse side of the first screen on the right. On the entrance wall is a large picture of 'Justice between St Michael and St Gabriel' by Jacobello del Fiore, and on the first screen on the left he and Michele Giambono are back to back, Giambono on the hither side with 'St James between two Evangelists and St George and St Alvise', Jacobello on the far side with the 'Madonna della Misericordia and Saints'. Just beyond, on an easel, is a pleasant little 'Virgin and Child' by Antonio Vivarini, but the other one by him on the screen nearby, of the 'Marriage of St Monica', is in a sad state. The second screen on the right has an 'Annunciation with two Saints' by Lorenzo Veneziano on the hither side, and on the far side, next to a 'Coronation of the Virgin' by Catarino, another picture by Lorenzo of the 'Mystical Marriage of St Catherine'. His also is the grand polyptych on the end wall.

In the centre of the room is a crystal and silver crucifix, 15th century, an exquisite piece of work with the Virgin, St John and St Mary Magdalene on the front and St Theodrore slaying the dragon on the reverse, all in the round, and the face and front of St Mary visible through the main crystal.

Room II

Nine pictures, four of them very good. Of the two by Giovanni Bellini, the 'Madonna Enthroned' is a fine, most dignified picture. On the left are St Francis, St John the Baptist and St Job and on the right St Louis (Lodovico), St Sebastian and St Dominic. St Job is there because the picture was painted for the church of S. Giobbe. Its date is doubtful, but a likely conjecture is about 1480. The other, the 'Mourning at the Foot of the Cross', is partly by Bellini and partly by his pupil, Rocco Marconi. It has recently been well cleaned. The two by Basaiti are excellent works of this artist, who started as a pupil of Alvise Vivarini and then became a follower in turn of Giovanni Bellini (as here), of Catena and of Giorgione. The better of the two is the 'Agony in the Garden', the merit of which has survived conscientious but injudicious cleaning. Of the three Cimas, the 'Doubting Thomas' (with St Magnus) is much the best, though the others have attractive features including, in the 'Madonna of the Orange Tree', a fox, a donkey, a deer, a white rabbit, two partridges and a lion, and, in the foreground, wild strawberries, violets, dandelions, ivy and aquilegia. Of the two Carpaccios, the 'Presentation in the Temple' is superb, the other, 'Ten Thousand Martyrs', far inferior. Ruskin pointed out that the colour of the 'Presentation' is perfect in a quiet key. The lute-player in the centre of the base is familiar from many reproductions.

Room III

Pass through this room quite quickly. The picture on the easel in the window, which was once attributed to Giorgione, but is now thought to be by Palma Vecchio or by Sebastiano del Piombo in his Giorgionesque manner, is worth a passing glance. On the far wall is the last damaged and faded fragment of Giorgione's frescoes once on the outer walls of the Fondaco dei Tedeschi. On either side of it are two quite good pictures by Cima, the 'Deposition' on the left, and on the right the 'Virgin between St John the Baptist and St Paul'.

Room IV

Here are a few excellent non-Venetian pictures together with two by Jacopo Bellini and some fine altar-pieces (though not the best) by Giovanni Bellini. The small Mantegna of St George is as good as can be. The saint is in black well-articulated armour with a burnished halo and stands in the artist's favourite landscape mostly of stratified rock. His red straps, scabbard and cloak and the red ribbons and cherries in the garland above balance the subdued green, blue and light brown that are the pervading colours. The Piero della Francesca was painted during a visit to Venice and,

though not one of his greatest works, shows all his merits. The Tura is typical, and whether you like Tura (one of the leading Ferrarese painters) is up to you. The Memling is interesting as a link between Flemish and Italian painting of the 15th century, because it was once thought to be by Antonello da Messina, who probably learned oil painting from the Flemish in Naples and introduced it to the Venetians on a visit to Venice.

Jacopo Bellini, the father of Gentile and Giovanni, learned from Gentile da Fabriano, who travelled from Florence and taught where he travelled, and Jacopo's two pictures here show his master's 'Gothic' influence. Of the Giovanni Bellinis the tender and strangely lit 'Madonna with St Mary Magdalene and St Catherine' is the outstanding one. In the other group St Paul is on one side of the Madonna and the saint in black armour on the other side is presumably St George but is unheroic enough to be a portrait of the donor.

6 Accademia. 'Coronation of the Virgin' by Paolo Veneziano

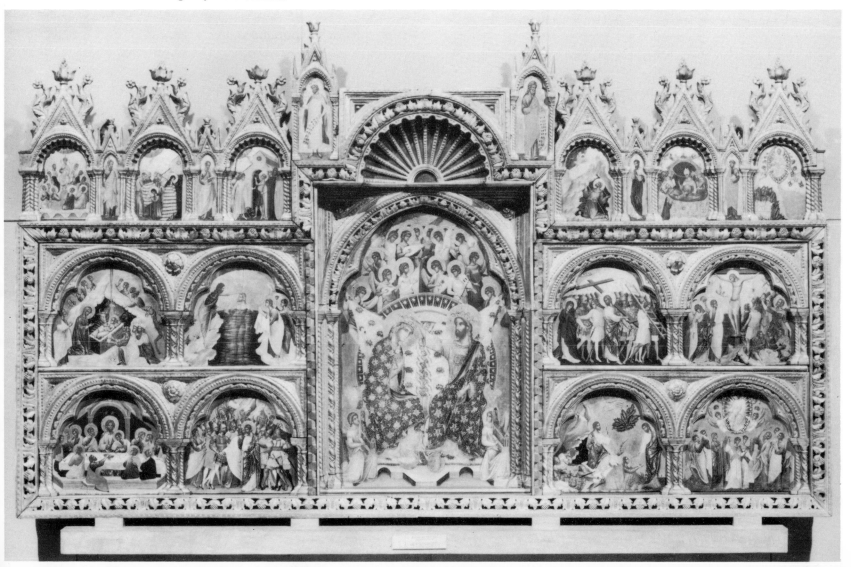

Of the two of the 'Madonna and Child', that in which the Madonna is 'in adoration' is early enough to show family influence.

Room V

This is the best room in the Gallery. There are three marvellous pictures by Giovanni Bellini. The 'Madonna degli Alberetti', so called because of the trees that flank the Virgin, has been damaged by two or three bad restorations, but is still one of Bellini's finest and most moving Madonnas. It is dated 1487 and the best of all Giovanni's models for the Virgin (we see her again in the Frari and at Murano) is used for the first time, looking sad but serene. The 'Pietà' is, to my mind, a great tragic masterpiece. Here again restorers have done their evil work and have partially ruined the face of the Madonna. But the infinitely sorrowful group of the dead Christ on His Mother's knees and the exquisite landscape (in which incidentally there are recognizable buildings at Ravenna and Vicenza) are typical of Giovanni Bellini's ability to combine deep dramatic feeling with pure beauty, and they make nonsense of a tendency in the past to doubt that the picture was painted by him. The light-blue picture with the Madonna between St Mary Magdalene and St John the Baptist is delightful, and is attributed without reservation to Bellini by Berenson and nearly all other modern experts. The 'Allegories' by Bellini were painted to decorate a Restello, some sort of table ornament that supported a mirror. Several unsuccessful attempts have been made to explain the subjects and it is better not to worry about them but simply to admire the supremely delicate painting. They are late works of his.

On either side of the 'Madonna degli Alberetti' are two other Madonnas by him, both early, the weak one on the right seeming not to have been painted from a model.

There remain the two pictures by Giorgione, of which the 'Tempesta' is one of the few established works of this rarest and greatest of painters. Here again what the subject is no one knows, but this is the first purely lyrical picture ever painted, a creation of mood and colour which says all it has to say in terms of poetry. It was slightly spoilt by a 19th century restoration which took paint off the woman's breast and her cape, but otherwise it is in surprisingly good condition. The other, 'La Vecchia', an old hag, was not always attributed to Giorgione, but was well cleaned in 1948

and since then has justified its attribution to him by its style and quality.

Room VI

The major work here is Tintoretto's 'Madonna dei Camerlenghi' or 'dei Tesorieri'. The subject is the 'Adoration of the Magi', here represented by three chamberlains (camerlenghi) who commissioned the picture. It is, as Ruskin observed, fairly absurd, they being dressed in their court clothes on one side and the Madonna being attended on the other by St Sebastian, St Mark and young St Theodore. But the composition, on a long, low canvas, is highly ingenious, the Madonna is strong and handsome, the background is luminous, and the portraits, in Tintoretto's most Titianesque manner, are first class.*

The 'Assumption of the Virgin', which is usually also in this room, is by Tintoretto, or mostly by him. The scene called 'Dives and Lazarus', with an architectural background and a group of musicians, is by Bonifazio Pitati, and thought by some to be his masterpiece. And the 'Fisherman giving the Doge the Ring of St Mark' is perhaps both the best and the best known picture by Paris Bordone.

Also, on the end wall, there is a well-painted but totally uninspired full-length picture of 'St John the Baptist' by Titian, which used to be on an easel in Room X and so is placed there by most guide-books. It is no doubt a portrait of someone who commissioned Titian to paint him as the Baptist.

Rooms VII, VIII and IX

In Room VII, on the right by the window, is a thoroughly attractive portrait of a young man by Lorenzo Lotto. It is beautifully painted and at first sight looks almost like an outstanding early 19th century French painting. Next to it is a pleasant picture, in subdued tones, by Savoldo, of 'St Antony and St Paul the Hermit'. In Room VIII is a fine set-piece, 'Sacra Conversazione', by Palma Vecchio, which he did not finish but Titian did, the Catharine's head being undoubtedly by the latter, also the 'Nativity' and the 'Crucifixion' by Andrea Previtali. In Room IX, if you like

*'As a piece of portraiture and artistical composition, the work is almost perfect. The sky appears full of light, though it is as dark as the flesh of the faces; and the forms of the floating clouds, as well as of the hills over which they rise, are drawn with a deep remembrance of reality.... There are hundreds of pictures of Tintoretto's more amazing than this, but I hardly know one that I more love.' J.R.

'Tobias and the Angel', there is a version of this subject from the school of Titian facing you as you enter.

Room X
This room has treasures in it. First of all, on the right, is the huge painting by Paolo Veronese which represents the 'Last Supper' and was first so-called. But he changed the name to 'The Feast in the House of Levi' when he was hauled before the Inquisition for having included Germans, dogs, a dwarf and a monkey in the representation of his holy subject. As you can see, he had amazing mastery of relieving foreground figures and objects against those in the middle distance and so on, creating aerial perspective, and all in the lightest key and most harmonious colouring. Also his sense of design was brilliant enough to make a perfect composition out of the innumerable parts of his vast picture.

On the wall facing the entrance is Tintoretto's first masterpiece, the 'Miracle of the Slave', full of colour and life and ingenious composition.* Recent cleaning has revealed the brilliance of its tone and lighting. Opposite it is Titian's last, which he did not finish, a 'Pietà' painted in his old age to hang, so he hoped, over the altar in the Frari in front of which he wished to be buried. As is written on the base of the picture, Palma Giovane finished it, but luckily he did so reverently and without spoiling his master's work, except for the heavy and insecure angel with a torch, which is his painting. The luminosity that derives from the broken light and shade in the painting looks forward to the Impressionists. Next to this on the right is a 'Crucifixion' by Tintoretto, not as marvellous as the one in San Rocco, but a great picture. Also by him are a 'Pietà' and 'Vision of St Jerome', both of which are good. The 'Dream of St Mark', the 'Presentation of the Virgin', 'Rescue at Sea' and the 'Apparition of the Virgin to two red-robed Saints' are less good, and the 'Stealing of the Body of St Mark', with lightning and an appalling camel, is one of his worst failures. The portrait by him on the easel, of the aged Procurator Soranzo, is as brilliant a portrait as can be. It is, however, thought by some reliable critics to be by Titian in his Tintorettesque manner.

Room XI

On the right are five pictures in a row by Tintoretto. The centre one, the 'Creation of Animals', is really rather bad, but the other two pairs, 'Adam and Eve' and 'Cain and Abel' (recently cleaned), which are early works, and 'St George and St Louis' and 'St Andrew and St Jerome', are of truly outstanding quality. Ruskin said that he would rather have these four pictures than 'all the other small pictures in Venice put together which he painted in bright colours for altarpieces; but I never saw . . . pictures which so nearly represented grisailles as these, and yet were delicious pieces of colour'.

Above them are pleasant ceiling pictures by Veronese, 'St Francis', 'St Nicholas at Myra' and 'Venice receiving Gifts from Hercules and Ceres'. All but one of the rest of the pictures in this part of the room are by him, and the best are the 'Annunciation' and the 'Madonna Enthroned' (both recently cleaned), next the 'Mystical Marriage of St Catherine' and the 'Battle of Lepanto', and least good the 'Coronation of the Virgin', the 'Assumption' and the 'Crucifixion'. In the 'Annunciation' there is on the balustrade on the right a vase with a rose-spray in it which is quite beautifully painted (it is worth going close to see how) and for which Ruskin said he would give all the bushes, trees and seas of Claude and Poussin.

In the further part of the room are ceiling pictures by G.B. Tiepolo, 'The Brazen Serpent' (an early work badly rubbed and scored) and 'St Helena finding the True Cross', one of his masterpieces. The gragments in the corners, also by him, are from the chapel in the Scalzi which was bombed in 1915. On the left wall is a good picture of 'St Jerome' by Jacopo Bassano, unless it is on an easel in the other part of the room, and there are two striking pictures by Luca Giordano of Naples, the 'Deposition' and the 'Crucifixion of St Peter'.

Corridor XII

Venetian 18th century landscapes by Francesco Zuccarelli, Marco Ricci (nephew of Sebastiano) and Giuseppe Zais, a follower of both the other two.

Room XIII

Tintoretto's picture of four senators, all strong portraits, with a weak Madonna and Child on the left of them, is now here, having been for years in Room XI. There are also portraits by him and three attractive pairs of small pictures by Andrea Schiavone.

Room XIV

This is given over to three Caravaggiesque painters, Bernardo Strozzi, Domenico Feti and Jan Lis.

Corridor XV

The most notable pictures here are a 'Vision of St Gaetanus' and 'The Infant Christ with St Joseph, St Anne and St Gaetanus', but not Virgin Mary, both by G. B. Tiepolo. There are also 'Abraham and the Angels' by his son, the 'Annunciation' by Pittoni, and 'Painting' and 'Sculpture' by G. A. Pellegrini.

Room XVI

Four very early Tiepolos: 'Diana and Actaeon', the 'Rape of Europa', 'Diana and Calypso' and 'Apollo and Marsyas'.

*The Slave was a Christian, put to punishment for going to St Mark's house to worship. St Mark, in the air, has foiled, and is foiling, the executioner. The spectator half in the picture on the left is said to be Tommaso Rangone (see S. Zulian), and, if it is, he must have commissioned the picture.

8
Accademia. 'Pietà'
by Titian

Room XVIA

This little room is dominated by Piazzetta's 'Fortune-Teller' (L'Indovina). Beside it is a successful anecdotal picture of a wounded man being treated by a surgeon, by an otherwise unknown 18th century painter called Gaspare Traversi. There are also portraits, some by Alessandro Longhi, the best by Domenico Pellegrini.

Room XVII

In the first section is the only picture by Canaletto in Venice, a beautiful capriccio of a courtyard and loggia. Also 'San Giorgio' by Francesco Guardi, a smaller 'Isola d'Anconetta', now rightly ascribed to him, and the 'Scuola di San Marco' by Bernardo Belloto, Canaletto's nephew and pupil.

In the second section there are a 'Crucifixion' by Piazzetta, the 'Dream of Aesculapius' by Sebastiano Ricci and the 'Adoration of the Magi' and the 'Last Supper' either by him or by Fontebasso. Also by Tiepolo, a sketch of the 'Glory of St Dominic' and the 'Miracle of the Man Sick of the Palsy', both early works, and two small pictures by Pittoni.

In the third section is an oil sketch by Tiepolo of the 'Transportation of the Holy House to Loreto', done for his picture in the Scalzi Chapel destroyed by a bomb (see Roman XI). There are also pastel portraits by Rosalba Carriera and six bright little pictures by Pietro Longhi, including a 'Concert', a 'Dancing Lesson' and a 'Chemist's Shop'.

Corridor XVIII
Here there are a 'Philosopher' by Longhi and small terracotta models by Canova in a glass case.

Corridor XIX
The best by far of the pictures by Basaiti is his well-painted 'Dead Christ'. At the end of the left is a quiet but moving 'Meeting of Joachim and Anna' by Carpaccio, which deserves to be hung in a better place. Opposite it is a strange picture by him of a procession of martyrs carrying crosses, a vision seen by a priest who had prayed to them during a plague.

From the window at the end you can see Palladio's facade in the courtyard, plain and built of brick in Doric, Ionic and Corinthian orders.

Room XX
The four principal pictures here have to do with the Relic of the Cross in the Scuola di S. Giovanni Evangelista, for which they were painted. The 'Procession of the Relic in the Piazza San Marco' is by Gentile Bellini and is dated 1496. The Doge and Signoria are watching the procession, whose head has entered St Mark's. The Campanile has been set to one side to show the Porta della Carta and the corner of the Doge's Palace, and is attached, as it was then, to an old Venetian-Byzantine building, now gone and to the original low Procuratie. On the other side of the picture you can see that the clock-tower was not yet built. On St Mark's are the original mosaics.

The other picture by Gentile Bellini himself shows the relic miraculously floating when it fell into the canal off the bridge of San Lorenzo. Heading the women is Caterina Cornaro, Queen of Cyprus, wearing her crown.

Partly by Gentile and partly by his assistants is the picture representing a man being cured of ague by being touched by a taper that has previously touched the Relic. It has suffered from damage and restoration.

The fourth picture was painted by Carpaccio in 1494. It represents a miraculous cure effected by the Archbishop of Grado with the Relic. The scene is the Rialto with the drawbridge that then existed. Carpaccio is the dog-lovers'

painter, and here you can see a rather ridiculous dog in one of the gondolas.

Room XXI
This contains Carpaccio's St Ursula series.

These pictures were painted between 1490 and 1500 for the Guild of St Ursula. In 1647 they were placed in a newly built school and some were cut to fit their new positions. In 1752 they were restored and partly repainted. Nevertheless they are mainly in fairly good preservation.

St Ursula, according to legend, was the daughter of Maurus, King of Brittany. The King of England, having heard of her beauty and wisdom, sent ambassadors to ask her father for her hand in marriage to his son Conon. The trouble was that Ursula and her father were Christians but the King of England and his son were heathens. It was arranged that Conon should be baptized and that he should marry Ursula after she had gone on a pilgrimage to Rome with several bishops and thousands of virgins, probably converts from England. After they saw the Pope they went, on their return journey, to Cologne, where they were all martyred by the Huns.

The first picture, which is opposite the door, shows the 'English Ambassadors at the Court of Brittany', and Ruskin says that 'the five principal figures on the right cannot be surpassed in Italian work for realistic portraiture'. He also greatly admired the embroidered tapestry behind them.

The second represents 'King Maurus giving assent to the 'Ambassadors', and Ruskin says that it is the most beautiful piece of painting in the series.

The third shows 'The King of England receiving the Favourable Reply from the Ambassadors'. The architecture, invented, but in Roman, Genoese and mainly Venetian styles, is magnificent, and so is the distance with its arches and water, flags and a tree-covered hill. Ruskin says that Carpaccio has been playful in his treatment of the subject, for instance in the King's keeping the ambassadors waiting while he finishes his previous business. But 'he is in the most vital and conclusive sense a man of genius who will not supply sublimity and pathos to order, but is sublime, delightful, dull or grotesque, as the humour takes him'. In the foreground on the right is an ape dressed up, sitting on the steps, and on the left, a rather charming boy with a fiddle.

9 Accademia. 'King of England receiving the Favourable Reply' by Carpaccio

The fourth is in four parts, the left and largest being 'Conon taking leave of his Father before his Embarkation', then his meeting with Ursula, and on the far right the two of them kneeling before Maurus, with the actual embarkation in the background. It is a picture full of incident, buildings and people.

The fifth is 'St Ursula's Dream of her Martyrdom', the angel appearing to her with the martyr's palm and a fillet, a Greek symbol also of victory. This is the best known of the series and usually the best liked, with several charming touches that supplement its high pictorial value.

The sixth, the 'Arrival of the Prince and Ursula in Rome', and their being received by the Pope, is, in Ruskin's view, the most beautiful after the 'Dream'. The Castle of St Angelo is put in to show that it is Rome. It is said that the Pope is a portrait of Alexander VI (Borgia).

The seventh picture, no doubt the worst, and this is not only Ruskin's opinion, was the first to be painted. It represents the arrival of the party, which now includes the Pope (an invention of Carpaccio's, for this is not in the legend), in Cologne.

The eighth depicts the martyrdom of all the pilgrim party by the Huns, with the funeral of Ursula on the right. It has suffered most of all from damage and restoration.

Lastly, the ninth picture, on the wall on the left of the entrance, is the 'Apotheosis of St Ursula'. 'The landscape and architecture are unsurpassably fine', says Ruskin, 'the rest much imperfect, but containing nobleness only to be learned by long dwelling on it.'

Carpaccio painted these pictures as space became available on the walls for which they were commissioned, and was probably twenty-five when he started them. First he did the two 'Arrivals', the 'Martyrdom' and the 'Apotheosis', which are clearly the least mature. Then came the brilliant 'Embarkation' and the serene 'Dream' and finally the three episodes of the Ambassadors (virtually a prologue), in which his pictorial and technical skills are marvellously combined.

(Room XXII is an empty passage.)

Room XXIII
This contains pictures of varying merit by Gentile and Giovanni Bellini, Crivelli and others.*

Room XXIV
Titian's 'Presentation of the Virgin'. Ruskin compared this unfavourably with Tintoretto's rather similar version of the same subject in the Church of the Madonna dell'Orto, but no other serious critic has disparaged it.

*This room is often cleared of its pictures and used for special exhibitions. When pictures are there, they may be some only of those that once were the full contents of the room and may be in any order. But all are labelled.

10 Accademia. 'St Ursula's Dream' by Carpaccio

(Also in Index of Artists: *Room III* Catena; *Room VI* Licinio, Moretto, Palma Vecchio, Pitati; *Room VIII* Marconi, Palma Vecchio, Pitati; *Room IX* Pitati; *Room XI* Mattei, Strozzi; *Room XIII* Bassano, Palma Giovarne; *Room XX* Bastiani, Diana, Mansueti; *Room XXIV* Antonio Vivarini and d'Alemagna; exterior B. Bon.)

Sant' Alvise   W Can: 5

A very old Gothic church, consecrated before 1400, now rather run down, with only a small statue of St Louis,* over the door, left from the original early 15th century exterior decoration. Inside, over the entrance wall is a 'barco', or monks' gallery, with its original early 15th century pillars topped by cross-pieces called 'barbacani'. The grille of the barco is 18th century. Over the pillars are two 16th century statues, and there are two more on either side of the altar on the right of the nave, on which is a painted wooden effigy of St Louis.

The principal pictures are three by Tiepolo, two in the corner, beyond the altar, of 'The Scourging of Christ', and 'Christ Crowned with Thorns', and a larger one, in the right wall of the chancel, of 'Christ Falling on the Road to Calvary'. Whether or not they were intended to form a triptych, they are more or less contemporaneous early works (the 'Road to Calvary' was painted in 1741, two years after the other two) and all demonstrate how, at this stage at any rate, when Tiepolo wanted to be deeply emotional he was in the result highly theatrical.

On the entrance wall, just over the font, is a portrait of a priest by Jacobello del Fiore, a fragment from a picture painted in 1402, and over it are eight crude but pleasant little pictures which would never have attracted much notice if Ruskin had not made the bizarre suggestion that they might have been painted by Carpaccio when he was a child. They are certainly in a childish or very simple amateurish style. The subjects are 'Nebuchadnezzar's Dream' (Daniel I), 'Solomon and the Queen of Sheba', 'Tobias and the Angel',

'Rachel at the Well', 'The Golden Calf', 'Joseph and his Brethren', 'Joshua before Jericho' and 'Job'. The 17th century ceiling painting, by A. Torri and P. Ricchi, came in for violent criticism from Ruskin, who said unfairly that it was Veronese's fault, on the grounds that, if he had not painted as he did, later derivative artists would not have painted like this.

(Also in Index of Artists: Paolo Veneziano.)

Sant' Andrea della Zirada   SC 1

This church is just off the Piazzale Roma and so is submerged by large modern buildings. It has a 15th century Gothic façade with two little 14th century bas-reliefs in the lunette over the door. Above is a skilful 'Dead Christ', below, by a cruder hand, a naive depiction of the 'Calling of Peter and Andrew'. A Venetian rowlock is on the boat and a Venetian oar floats in the foreground.

Inside, the 'barco', or nuns' gallery, over the door, is 15th century, but the two columns that support it (with barbacani, or cross-pieces, at the tops) are survivals from the first 14th century building, which was otherwise demolished and replaced about 1450. The elaborate decoration on the barco was added in the 17th century, and while the wrought ironwork is tasteful, the cherubs and the rest are flagrantly unsuitable for a church. The church has been closed and is let by the Comune to a sculptor as a studio.

Angelo Raffaelle   WD 2

The organ screen is beautifully decorated with pictures of the story of Tobias by either Francesco or Giovanni Antonio Guardi. On the right wall is 'St Francis receiving the Stigmata' by Palma Giovane.

The church is in the angle of two canals, its own Rio on the north and another coming up from San Sebastiano on the east. Where they meet, on the north bank of the former, stands the Palazzo Ariani, the best surviving example of the first Gothic architecture in Venice, with eastern influence in its lovely traceried windows.

Sant' Antonino   W Cas: 15

Perhaps designed by Longhena. Contains a poor 'Deposition' by Bastiani in the chapel on the right of the chancel, and a bust of the Procurator Alvise Tiepolo, by Vittoria, in the Saba chapel on the left of the nave, the walls and ceiling of

11 Angelo Raffaelle. 'Tobias' (detail) by Guardi

which are painted by Palma Giovane with episodes in the life of St Antonino.

Sant' Apollinare (usually called S. Aponal)   SP 8
This church, which contains nothing of importance and is never open, has a very fine 15th century Gothic facade with a 14th century bas-relief of the Crucifixion and some earlier reliefs on it. The campanile dates from the 13th century, but was renovated in the 15th.

Santi Apostoli   E Can: 4
The main chapel on the right is that of the Corner family, and in it are the recumbent figures of two of them on sarcophagi. Its design and date are such that it may be by Guglielmo dei Grigi or Mauro Coducci. On its altar is one of Tiepolo's most successful religious paintings, the 'Communion of St Lucy', later (1746-8) than his pictures in S. Alvise and less melodramatic.

In the chapel on the right of the chancel are the remains of early 14th century Venetian-Byzantine frescoes, and also a bas-relief of the head of St Sebastian, by Tullio Lombardo, a fine thing. On the left wall of the chancel is a large picture of 'The Fall of Manna', started by Veronese and finished by someone else. In the chapel on the left of the chancel is a strange, attractive picture of an angel leading a child by the hand, by Francesco Maffei.

Arsenale   W Cas: 18
The main gateway was built in 1460 to Gambello's design, and the figure of 'St Justina' on the coping is a later addition by Campagna. The lions in front of the gate are Greek, and the two closest to it were brought back from Athens after Venice reconquered the Peloponnese in 1687. That on the left has Runic inscriptions on it, attributed to some Scandinavian mercenaries in the Byzantine army. It was originally at the Piraeus, and the main inscription starts 'Hakon, with Ulf and Asmund and Orn, captured this port'.

Galleria d'Arte Moderna, Palazzo Pesaro   SC 7
This Palazzo was built between 1660 and 1710. It was designed by Longhena, but he died in 1682, and Antonio Gaspare modified his design for the facade on the Grand Canal. The courtyard and open ground floor are imposing, and in the former, standing on an earlier well-head, is a statue of Apollo by Danese Cattaneo, a pupil of Sansovino.

The collection of modern art starts on the second floor with three rooms (or two rooms and the Hall) taken up by Italian 19th century painters. In the remaining six rooms are works by modern Italian and foreign artists. They are sometimes moved but they are all labelled and so can be found if the following (1971) arrangement is wrong:

Room IV
Bonnard (a bright nude), Corot, Luce, Ben Nicholson (a fine abstract called 'Venomous Yellow', under glass and hung in the worst position between two windows), Permeke, Le Sidaner, Zadkine and Jean Arp.

Room V
Chagall (a striking portrait of a Rabbi), Derain (a fine landscape), Marquet, Nolde, Rouault, Vlaminck, Zadkine again and Bourdelle.

Back in the Hall
A ballerina and two female heads by Emilio Greco, some more Italian pictures and plaster casts of Rodin's 'Penseur' and 'Burghers of Calais'.

Room VI
Eduardo Chillida, Max Ernst, Kandinsky, Klee and Mark Tobey, Lynn Chadwick and Henry Moore.

Rooms VII and IX
Campigli, Di Chirico, Matisse, Miro and Arturo Tosi (all given by Lidia di Lisi in memory of her husband Lionello) and Morandi, De Pisis and Sironi.

Down on the first floor the central hall, *Room XI,* is used for special exhibitions and has no permanent contents of any interest.

Room XII
Prints, including some by Ensor, Matisse, Munch and Odilon Redon.

Room XIII
This has ceiling pictures and a frieze representing the 'Glories of the Pesaro Family' by Nicolo Bambini. On its walls are Charles Shannon, Lavery and William Nicholson in a row, but its main work is a delightful stone figure of a 'Crouching Woman' by Emilio Greco.

12A San Bartolomeo. 'St Louis' (S. Alvise) by Sebastiano del Piombo

12B San Bartolomeo, 'St Sebald' (S. Sinibaldo) by Sebastiano del Piombo

Room XIV

On the ceiling is a humdrum painting of 'Jupiter' by Pittoni. Also there are several pictures by Guglielmo Ciardi, and some by Sironi.

Room XV

More Ciardis, a good sad 'Eve' in bronze by Francesco Massima, and one of Manzu's cardinals.

Room XVI

Nothing of interest.

Room XVII

Arturo Martini.

Remaining Rooms

A 'Broken Disc', of merit, by Pomodoro, an abstract sculpture by Umberto Milani and works by Medardo Rosso.

San Barnaba WD 6

Mid 18th century, but tucked behind it on the north side is a 13th century campanile. Over the last altar on the left wall of the nave is a charming small picture of 'The Holy Family', considered by Berenson to be an early work by Veronese.

San Bartolomeo R 4

This is a 12th century building fully restored and redecorated in 1723. It contains two double pictures that were once organ doors, painted by Sebastiano del Piombo before he left Venice for Rome in 1511, and therefore while he was under the influence of Giorgione. The pair on the wall between the first two altars on the right of the nave, of 'St Bartholomew' and 'St Sebastian', are good enough, but the pair in the corresponding position near the side door in the left wall of the nave, through which you enter the church, are truly magnificent. They are of 'St Louis' (S. Alvise) and 'St Sebald' (S. Sinibaldo).*

*St Bartholomew would naturally be a saint to depict in his own church and St Sebastian is always popular with painters, especially those called Sebastiano. St Louis, who is briefly described in the footnote to the church of San Alvise above, is fairly popular. But St Sebald is the patron saint of Nuremberg, where his shrine is and where he lived as a hermit and worked several miracles, including using icicles successfully as fuel on the fire of a poor man who was giving him shelter and was out of wood. Why he is portrayed (as he is here) as a pilgrim, is obscure. Why he is portrayed here at all is just as obscure, one small clue being, however, that his day is the same as that of St Louis, 19 August.

The 'Fall of Manna' over the sacristy door is by Sante Peranda, and 'The Virgin and St Francis Xavier' in the chapel on the left of the chancel is by Balestra. There are also three pictures by Palma Giovane, a huge, bad one, of 'The Plague of Serpents' on the left wall of the nave, next to 'St Matthew' by Corona, and on either side of the chancel 'St Bartholomew baptizing the King and Queen of Armenia' on the left, a heavy painting, clumsily restored, and on the right, rather less ponderous, 'St Bartholomew assaulted by Ruffians'. All of these are perishing from neglect, and the Balestra is probably beyond repair.

Capella di San Basso SM 14

This is what this little building in the Piazzetta dei Leoncini is now called. It was once the 'Chiesa' di San Basso, but it has long been disused for church purposes and de-consecrated, being now a lecture hall and a repository for some of the works of art belonging to St Mark's. Entry is by application to the doorkeeper of the Palazzo Patriarcale at the east end of this same Piazzetta, he being custodian of the key.

The Capella dates from about 1670, and architecturally is pleasant inside and out. To it have now been transferred the organ screens by Gentile Bellini that used to be in the Museo Marciano. They were painted in his youth and in a very Mantegnesque style, and once the pair representing 'St Mark' and 'St Theodore' were labelled as being by Mantegna. The other two, labelled as by Gentile Bellini, are of 'St Jerome' and 'St Francis'.

San Benedetto SM 1

A small church, seldom open. The main picture on the right, of 'St Sebastian having his Wounds washed by Holy Women', by Bernardo Strozzi, is boldly painted. On the left, nearest the door, is a rather faded and over-cleaned picture of 'St Francis of Paola' by Tiepolo, which has unusual dignity and is skilfully composed. Collectors of rarities may like to study the two pictures by Sebastiano Mazzoni on the walls flanking the chancel, one of 'St Benedict presenting a Priest to the Virgin', the other of 'St Benedict in Glory with St John the Baptist'.

(Also in Index of Artists: Fumiani, Guarana.)

The Palazzo Pesaro (or degli Orfei, or Fortuny) dominates the little square outside the church. It is Venetian-Gothic, early 15th century with a few late 15th century additions, and one of the finest palazzi not on the Grand Canal. The

S · THEODORVS ·

13A   San Basso. 'St Theodore'
by Gentile Bellini

facade on the other side of it (go down the alley on the right of it to the Ponte S. Michiel) is plainer but architecturally impeccable. So splendid a building deserves to be kept in better condition.

The Bovolo   SM 10

A very handsome exterior spiral staircase built as part of the Palazzo Contarini in or about 1500 by some Lombard architect. A 'bovolo' is a snail shell, which is more or less spiral.

Burano See Torcello.

Cà D'Oro   E Can: 2

This is the best-known and the finest small Venetian Gothic building in the city. It was called the 'House of Gold' because the decoration on the front of it facing the Grand Canal was originally lavishly gilded. It is worth a visit because it is beautiful architecturally inside and out* and contains some attractive furniture, objets d'art and coins, but its pictures are not so good, and you need not allow as much time for it as the number of them might seem to require. It was built between 1420 and 1434 and may have been completed under the direction of Giovanni and Bartolomeo Bon.

The courtyard into which you enter is a pretty one, with a 15th century well-head by Bartolomeo Bon and a handsome staircase up which you climb to the first floor. In the long hall there are, against the wall which faces you as you enter, four busts, three of them by Vittoria. Farther along on the same wall there used to be a bas-relief in the form of a lunette by Sansovino, but it has been removed.

Room I is on the left as you go along the hall, at the end, looking over the Grand Canal, as does the open loggia at its side. The pictures on the entrance wall of the 'Annunciation' and 'Death of the Virgin' are partly by Carpaccio but partly by his pupils and not very good. On the same wall are two bronze bas-reliefs of battles, one between centaurs and giants and the other between horsemen and foot soldiers, by Gambello. On the opposite wall are four bronze bas-reliefs of the 'Story of the Cross' by Riccio.

Room II leads off Room I and has in it a fine wooden staircase, of the 15th century. *Room III* is on the other side of the hall next to the loggia. It has, standing forward from the entrance wall, on the right, a marble bas-relief of busts of a young man and a young woman by Tullio Lombardo. By the window on the right is quite an attractive bust of a young boy, ascribed to Gian Crisostomo Romano (or even to Francesco Laurana, by whom it certainly is not). And, standing forward from the entrance wall on the left, there is a good bust by Vittoria of an old priest. In *Room IV,* next to this, the picture of 'Venus' is attributed to Titian by some, but not by me, nor indeed by Berenson. On the wall on the right nearest the window is a pleasant Florentine picture of the 'Virgin in Adoration' by Botticini and, in the centre of the entrance wall, another Florentine painting of the 'Virgin and the Infant St John in Adoration' by Jacopo del Sellaio. In *Room V,* the next one on this side, the 'Madonna and Child' is not by Giovanni Bellini but is a weak effort by one of his pupils. In the small chapel which adjoins this room, so being labelled *Room VI,* is the pride of the collection, a late, unfinished picture by Mantegna of 'St Sebastian'. It may be the last picture that Mantegna painted. At the bottom of it is a lighted candle, and, on a scroll attached to it, Latin words meaning 'Nothing is stable except what is divine, the rest is smoke'. The ceiling of the chapel is fine 15th century woodwork.

On the second floor, in the recess corresponding to the Mantegna chapel on the first floor, is a competent portrait by Van Dyck painted during a visit to Venice. Also a grand gilt terracotta bust of the Procurator Marino Grimani by Vittoria. The rooms on this floor are numbered in reverse order to those below, and so, this recess being *VII,* the room next to it, which contains nothing of interest, is *Room VIII.* The next, *Room IX,* has a handsome ceiling and a fair picture of a shy young girl by Pontormo, all the rest being school pictures or pictures by indifferent minor artists. In *Room X* the picture of the 'Virgin between St Jerome and St Catherine' (half-length) is considered by Berenson to be a late work of Cima da Conegliano with plenty of studio assistance, but by others a masterpiece by Cima on his own. Berenson must seem right to anyone who has studied Cima. Equal doubt exists about the two little views of Venice in this same room, which may or may not be by Francesco Guardi. The 'Madonna and Child' by Giambono is interesting because he was an early Venetian, and it has a certain charm.

---

*Ruskin called it 'a noble pile of very quaint Gothic, once superb in general effect, but not destroyed by restorations'. These 19th century restorations have since been removed and the building put back as far as possible to its original state.

Across the hall in *Room XI* there are four 'sportelli' (small doors) by Riccio and, also by him, a splendid bronze bas-relief of 'St Martin dividing his cloak for the benefit of a Beggar'. There is nothing of the slightest interest in the adjoining *Room XII*.

Rooms XIII, XIV and *XV* are entered through the loggia on this floor, and in *Room XIII* are some excellent bronzes, including an 'Apollo' (partly gilt) by Antico, a bas-relief of 'The Deposition' by Riccio, a second one of the back of a cow by a Paduan called Bellano and a third, of three horses, ascribed either to him or, paradoxically, to a follower of Riccio. In *Room XV* are maquettes by Bernini of the 'Nile' and the 'River Plate' and specimens from the coin collection, but the really good ones, by Pisanello, Pollaiuolo, Gentile Bellini and so on, are not always on view.

(Also in Index of Artists: *Room I* Antonio Vivarini, *Room II* Bordone, *Room V* Licinio, *Room VII* Bonifazio, *Room VIII* Alessandro Longhi, Palma Giovane, Domenico ·Tiepolo, *Room XI* Bonifazio, Diana, Domenico Tintoretto.)

15 The Bovolo

Cà Rezzonico

This is one of the most imposing palaces on the Grand Canal, designed and mostly built by Longhena in the middle of the 17th century, but completed a hundred years later, when the top storey was added, by the Rezzonico family. It was acquired by the City of Venice in 1935 and turned into a museum of 18th century Venetian pictures and furniture, with a good start provided by the decoration, including frescoes and painted ceilings, put in when the Rezzonico family took it over.

From the hall you ascend a grand staircase, with two rather coarse little figures of putti dressed as Autumn and Winter on the banisters, to the Piano Nobile and enter first the large and sumptuous ballroom, which spans the building. From this you go by the door on the tight into a series of rooms, the first of which has on the ceiling a bold and bright picture by Tiepolo of a 'Nuptial Allegory', in which a Rezzonico and his bride arrive in the Chariot of the Sun with Apollo and suitable attendants.

Down the small staircase from this room are some smaller ones which were used by the Rezzonico Pope, Clement XIII, and in which Robert Browning worked and died. In the end one are some of his books and possessions. In the yellow room are two small pictures sometimes ascribed to Pietro Longhi, but not in fact by him. Back to the Piano Nobile you pass from the 'Nuptial' Room into one that has some elaborate furniture and on its walls many pastels, the three on the wall facing you portraits by Rosalba Carriera. Next is the Tapestry Room and then the Throne Room, with a ceiling painting of 'Merit, Nobility and Virtue' by Tiepolo, rather faded, but an airy imaginative composition. You now cross to the other side of the building and enter the so-called Tiepolo Room, which has yet another luminous ceiling painting by him, this one of 'Strength and Widsom', and a portrait of an old man, also by him, to left of far door. Next come the Library, and the room called Lazzarini (because it has three pictures by that undistinguished artist) and then the Brustolon Room, named after the sculptor who designed much of the furniture in it. Lastly to the left there is the large hall which was crossed earlier and off which leads the staircase to the second floor. There are two statues by Vittoria in it, one on each side of the staircase door.

The similar hall on the second floor, into which you step from the stairs, is full of pictures, one of them, opposite the entrance door, a very large representation by Piazzetta of 'The Death of Darius', and another next to it, by G. Pellegrini, of 'Mucius Scaevola in the Camp of Lars Porsena', a light and facile thing. By the window there was once one of Piazzetta's self-portraits, but it was on loan and may not be returned, having been removed by the lender. In *Room XIV* are three frescoes subdued in tone but fine, of 'Minerva, Apollo and Venus', by Francesco Guardi, and in *Room XVIII* on the ceiling a 'Triumph of Diana' by him or his brother, Gian Antonio. In *Room XIX* is another ceiling-picture by Tiepolo, of 'Zephyrus and Flora', painted in his strong and brilliant manner, and on the walls over thirty little topical scenes by Pietro Longhi. On the left wall the three in the upper row on the right are two scenes of Prince Eugene of Savoy in camp and a portrait of an Irish giant called McGrath, and next to them a good portrait of Francesco Guardi, followed (to the left) by family groups. On the entrance wall are, above, masked ladies and, below, a miscellany including a rhinoceros. There are also some peasant scenes and, on the left wall, beyond the door, a 'Painter's Studio', and on the wall facing the entrance, between the windows, a rather charming picture of boys riding. *Room XX* has two vivid pictures, almost certainly by F. and G. A. Guardiin collaboration, one of the 'Gambling House' (Ridotto), the other of the 'Nuns' Room at S. Zaccaria'. *Rooms XXIII* to *XXIX* contain frescoes by Domenico Tiepolo, the best those in *Room XXVI*, all of 'Pagliacci', some in colour and some in grisaille.

(Also in Index of Artists: Guarana, Alessandro Longhi, Maffei, Zuccarelli.)

I Carmini (Church and School) See Santa Maria del Carmelo and Santa Maria del Carmine.

San Cassiano

A very old foundation but nothing survives later rebuilding except the 13th century campanile and some even earlier fragments around the door.

Inside, in the chapel on the right of the chancel, the 'Birth of St John' and 'Prediction to Zacharias' (both with donors) may well be by Jacopo Bassano. Round the High Altar are three pictures by Tintoretto. 'The Descent into Limbo', on the right, and 'The Resurrection', behind the altar, are both considerably restored. 'The Crucifixion', on the left, painted

16A   Cà Rezzonico, 'Boys Riding' by Pietro Longhi

in 1568, is an original and elaborately contrived composition, but is altogether lacking in emotion. Ruskin described it as being superbly painted, and notable for the modesty of its colour, of which he said 'not the slightest touch of it but is delicious'. He added that he considered the picture generally to be 'quite beyond all price'. But he was nearer the mark when he pointed out that the strange treatment of the scene seemed to indicate that Tintoretto painted this picture 'for his own delight' and so as to render 'the principals accessory, and the accessories principal'.

The picture on the right wall nearest the main entrance door, of 'St John the Baptist between St Peter, St Paul and

16B Cà Rezzonico, 'Pagliacci' by Domenico Tiepolo

two other Apostles', is probably by Palma Vecchio (but perhaps by Rocco Marconi) and, when cleaned, will be worth more than a passing glance. In the sacristy chapel the 'Martyrdom of St Cassian' by Balestra, and an altar-piece by Pittoni.

Museo Correr   SM 20

The entrance is the central way on the west into the Piazza San Marco. Up steep stairs you reach the first floor with twenty-four rooms of Venetiana, maps, Doges' robes, flags, books, coins, armour, model ships and so on. In *Room I* is the statue of 'Daedalus and Icarus' that made Canova's name as a young man. In *Room II* is (or used to be) a poor half-effaced picture ascribed to Catena but unrecognizable as his, and in *Room V* are two portraits of Doges by Bastiani on the same canvas. In *Room VI* is an attractive free version, attributed to Gian Antonio Guardi of the picture by Paris Bordone in the Accademia which represents a fisherman handing to the Doge the ring which he had miraculously been given by St Mark. In *Rooms VIII* and *IX* are rather mediocre portraits by Alessandro Longhi but in the latter is a picture of 'Three Treasurers and three Secretaries before St Justina', a well-painted piece of portraiture by Tintoretto. In *Room X* is a very pleasant picture, all red and rose, by Pietro Longhi, of a 'Doge giving Audience', and in *Room XIII* is a good bust of Admiral Duodo by Vittoria.

At the back of *Room XVI* another long, steep staircase leads up to the picture-gallery proper. All the pictures and objets d'art are labelled, and so those picked out below can easily be found.

Room 2
Two panels, each of three saints, by Paolo Veneziano.

Room 3
A polyptych and a picture of 'Christ surrounded by Saints', both by Lorenzo Veneziano.

Room 4
A statuette of Doge T. Mocenigo by J. Delle Masegne.

Room 6
The 'Virgin and Child with a Goldfinch' by Giambono, a fragment by Stefano da Zevio, of 'Angels', and another 'Virgin and Child' by Jacobello del Fiore.

Room 7
A 'Pietà' by Cosimo Tura.

Room 8
A portrait by Baldassare Estense (another Ferrarese painter) and two pictures of the 'Virgin and Child' by Bartolomeo Vivarini.

Room 9
Good small bronzes by Sansovino, Antico, Campagna, Roccatagliata and others. (Sometimes replaced by examples of Burano lace.)

Room 11
A good small 'Crucifixion' by Hugo van der Goes and a large partly spoiled 'Dead Christ' by Antonello da Messina that must once have been fine. Also a 'Virgin and Child' by Dirck Bouts.

Room 13
A small early 'Crucifixion' by Giovanni Bellini. Another, in the form of a predella, by Jacopo Bellini. A young saint with a laurel wreath, possibly by Giovanni Bellini, but not credited to him by Berenson. A rather weak 'Virgin and Child', a very moving 'Pietà' and a rather harsh 'Transfiguration', all by Giovanni Bellini and all early works. The 'Pietà' incidentally has a forged monogram of Dürer on it. Finally a profile portrait of Doge Giovanni Mocenigo, probably by Gentile Bellini.

Room 14
A delightful small 'St Antony of Padua' by Alvise Vivarini. Also a ruined Cima of the 'Virgin, St Laurence and St Nicholas' and the 'Virgin and Child and St Joseph' and 'St Justina', both by Montagna.

Room 15
On the wall 'St Peter Martyr' by Carpaccio, a rather ordinary picture, and on the easel 'Two Courtesans' by him, by no means ordinary, a first-class painting with some rather repellent features, which Ruskin once unwisely called 'the best picture in the world', a judgement ever since quoted against him.

17 Museo Correr. 'The Virgin and Child' by Lotto

Room 16
A 'Visitation' ascribed by Berenson to Carpaccio, but very weak for him, and a portrait of a man in a red hat also ascribed by Berenson to him.

Room 17
An enchanting 'Virgin and Child' by Lorenzo Lotto (Plate 17). Also a bronze bust ascribed to Riccio.

If, when you leave, you go out of the archway on the right (i.e. away from the Piazza) and turn right again, you will see facing you a 13th century building, the Albergo del Salvadego. It has been restored, but still shows early features, round-arched windows with pointed tops, a long loggia above with a projecting roof, and a pillared ground storey (converted into an office-front for an insurance company).

Sant' Elena   E Cas: 6
Late 15th century, a brick Gothic façade with a fine bas-relief by Rizzo over the door, representing the warrior Vittore Cappello kneeling before St Helen. The interior, which has recently been restored, has some good Gothic features, but the church is seldom open. The lunette presents a problem in connoisseurship. The figure of Vittore Cappello is unfinished on the left side which you cannot see, and is much more lifelike and tense than that of St Helena. This may be simply because the former was a portrait and the latter imaginary, or perhaps because only the former is Rizzo's and the latter is the work of an assistant. In any case the figures were once united by St Helena's Cross, which rose straight and high between them, with one hand of each holding it.

Sant' Eufemia   G 1
Frequently restored and so dateless, but the columns and their capitals are 11th century. Over the first altar on the right wall of the nave is a triptych, the centre picture of which, 'St Roch and an Angel', is by Bartolomeo Vivarini, as also is the 'Virgin and Child' in the lunette above it.

San Fantino   SM 9
Started by Scarpagnino, finished 1550-64 by Sansovino. A fine example, outside and inside, of simple early Renaissance architecture. On the right wall of the nave is the 'Deposition' by Palma Giovane, and on the left wall of the chancel a 'Thanksgiving for Lepanto' also by him. On the left wall of the nave the 'Visitation' is by Sante Peranda and the 'Crucifixion' by Leonardo Corona.

On the north of the church across the Calle dei Barcarolli is the Ateneo Veneto, built at the end of the 16th century under guidance from Vittoria. The statues of the Virgin and two Angels on the pediment and the Crucifix in relief in front of it are by his pupils. Inside the building, though it is hard to get inside, are an 'Assumption' by Veronese and 'St Jerome receiving Gifts' by Tintoretto, besides busts in bronze of three doctors by Vittoria.

San Felice   W Can: 12
1530-40. The last picture on the right wall of the nave represents 'St Demetrius and a Worshipper' and is by Tintoretto (early). On either side of the altar are statues of 'Hope' and 'Charity' by Giulio del Moro, late 16th century. Also by him are the bronzes of 'St Peter' and 'St John' on the walls of the chancel and 'The Madonna' on the left wall of the nave near the entrance door.

Fenice Theatre   SM 8
Built 1790-2. Rebuilt after a fire in 1836. The unattractive facade is all that remains of the first building. The interior is decorated in Venetian 18th century style and is enchanting.

Santa Fosca   W Can: 9
Early 18th century. On the left wall of the nave is the 'Holy Family and Donor' by Domenico Tintoretto. Below it, nearest the door, is a 15th or 16th century Greek painting of 'The Madonna between St John Chrysostom and St Joseph'. The handsome late 15th century campanile is, according to Ruskin, 'of late Gothic uninjured by restorations and peculiarly Venetian in being crowned with the cupola, not the pyramid'.

San Francesco di Paola   E Cas: 2
A rather dull late 16th century building. The interior was entirely redecorated in the 18th century, except for the ceiling, which is original. The paintings on it, which are not very good, are by Contarini, a pupil of Titian. The 'Annunciation' in the chapel right of the chancel is by Palma Giovane. On the left of the nave the 'Martyrdom of St Bartholomew' is by Marieschi, and one of the pictures on the cornice, the 'Healing of a Madman', is by Domenico Tiepolo.

18   San Francesco della Vigna, 'The Virgin in Adoration' by Negroponte

San Francesco della Vigna

This large remote church was designed by Sansovino, but its façade is by Palladio. The two statues on the façade stand out enough to attract notice, and so, though they are of negligible artistic value, let it be said that they are by T. Aspetti.

First to be noted inside are the bronzes over the holy-water stoups, 'St Francis' and 'St John the Baptist' by Vittoria. On the right there is nothing of importance until you come to the fourth altar where there is a 'Resurrection', possibly by Veronese though probably by, or partly by, a skilful pupil of his. Then round the corner in the right-hand chapel of the right transept is a large, pretty, rather primitive picture of the 'Virgin in Adoration' by Antonio da Negroponte, painted about 1450, and combining Gothic feeling with a certain concession to Renaissance form. Negroponte is a very rare painter, and this picture, which is undoubtedly his masterpiece, is a great favourite with Venice-lovers.

The High Altar in the chancel was put together by Longhena from parts of different dates but is quite handsome. In the main chapel next to it in the left-hand transept there are some good late 15th and early 16th century sculptures, the base-reliefs of prophets and the four Evangelists being by the Lombardi and their assistants. The door in this transept leads not only to the sacristy, in which there is nothing of importance, but also by a corridor to a small chapel near the cloisters which contains an attractive late picture of the 'Virgin and Child with Saints' by Giovanni Bellini, in which the figure of the donor was painted in later, and not by Bellini.

Back in the main church, in the chapel nearest the chancel (fifth from the entrance wall), is a good early picture by Paolo Veronese of the 'Holy Family with St Catherine and St Antony Abbot', whose pig is half hidden by St Catherine. In the next chapel but one the monochrome frescoes in the spandrels and roundels are by Tiepolo. And in the next after this the three statues are by Vittoria, the central one of 'St Antony Abbot' much better than the other two (Plate 19) and the same in design as his similar statue in S. Sebastiano. The bas-relief on this side of the entrance wall of the 'Virgin' is 12th century Byzantine.

(Also in Index of Artists: Palma Giovane, Domenico Tintoretto, Antonio Vivarini, Aspetti.)

The Frari (Santa Maria Gloriosa dei Frari)

The building of this huge church by the Franciscan friars lasted over a hundred years, having been started in 1340 and finished in 1443. It is, like SS. Giovanni e Paolo, a pure example of Venetian Gothic. The façade is simple and majestic, with a fine main doorway, over which the statue of Christ is by Vittoria or mainly by him. The figures of 'The Madonna', on the left, and 'St Francis', on the right, are 15th century.

Inside there are four masterpieces that deserve attention before anything else. First there are two great and famous pictures by Titian, the 'Assumption of the Virgin' over the high Altar, and the 'Pesaro Madonna' on the left wall of the nave.

The 'Assumption', which was finished in 1518, might easily be reckoned to be Titian's greatest work. Ruskin blew hot and cold about it, having first complained of too much 'fox colour', and warned us that it was 'not one whit the better for being either large or gaudy in colour', but he came to regard it as a very fine picture without any religious feeling in it. The friars who commissioned it complained that the apostles were too large, though Titian explained that they must be (as they are) in proportion to the vastness of the space. They only stopped criticizing when they had a large offer for the picture from Charles V. In fact the reds in it are pure red, and the Madonna, soaring in blue against the great dull gold circle rimmed by cherubs, has in the lower group a perfect contrast, with the raised arm of one of the Apostles a brilliantly apt last broken contact between her and the world.

Ruskin called the 'Pesaro Madonna' 'the best Titian in Venice', and pointed out that the whole, very successful, composition depends on the line of St Peter's key lying on the steps (Plate 20). He also expressed much more admiration than we can think due for the face of the young man looking straight out of the picture in the bottom right-hand corner. This young man and the others kneeling with him are members of the Pesaro family. The man kneeling on the left and being presented by St Peter to the Virgin is Jacopo Pesaro, a militant bishop of Paphos, who commissioned the picture, after defeating the Turks in a sea-battle, just after the 'Assumption' was finished. The Virgin, dignified and very beautiful, looks towards St Peter and the victorious bishop. The Infant Christ, linking the composition of the scene, smiles on the other group, who are under the tutelage of the dark-habited St Francis, a foil to the splendid colour of the

**19 San Francesco della Vigna. 'St Antony Abbot' and 'St Roch'
by Vittoria**

20 The Frari, The 'Pesaro Madonna' by Titian

rest of the picture. It was begun in 1519 and finished in 1525 (or 1526) and this date is important because for the first time an acknowledged master in a grand and sacred picture abandoned the traditional composition in which the Virgin was the central figure of a group. Through the success of this altar-piece, therefore, imaginative conception became a vital part of the development of European religious painting.

Next, in the first chapel on the right of the chancel is an unusual thing to find in Venice, a carved and painted wooden statue by Donatello. This is of 'St John the Baptist', wild and emaciated, very moving and almost alarming.

Finally, in the sacristy, over the altar, is a triptych by Giovanni Bellini which is of such perfect beauty that you can imagine him wondering when he had finished it whether there was anything left for him to do (Plate 21). In fact its date is 1488 and he painted many pictures after it, most in a freer style such as the altar-piece in S. Zaccaria and 'St Jerome' in S. Giovanni Crisostomo. But, though his works cover a wide range of subjects, he had always been striving particularly for perfection in the painting of altar-pieces, and in this picture he seems really to have achieved it. The saints in it are, on the left, St Nicholas with St Peter beyond him

21   The Frari. Triptych 'Madonna and Saints' by Giovanni Bellini

and, on the right, probably St Benedict with St Mark beyond him.

The Virgin is Bellini's lovely sad-eyed model of this period. All stiffness is taken out of the group by the turning of St Benedict's head towards us. On the left the description in reflected light of the vestments of St Nicholas is a marvel of accuracy and vivacity. Taine's comment was *'toutes ces figures ont vécu'*. The splendid contemporary frame is quite rightly signed by its maker, Jacopo da Faenza.

Now let us turn to the rest of the contents of the Frari. You enter by one of two doors. That in the end wall of the left transept may be in use, or else that which leads through a flamboyant late 17th century monument (to a Pesaro) halfway down the left side of the nave. Between these two doors there is first in the transept, near the choir, a holy-water stoup with a small bronze statue of 'St Francis' over it by Campagna. Then, in the Chapel of St Peter (or Emiliani), the entrance to which is just before Titian's 'Pesaro Madonna', there is a marble altar-piece and also a monument, both early 15th century and in the style of the Delle Masegne.

Beyond the 'Pesaro Madonna' is the Pesaro monument and its door, and next to them, going down the left wall of the nave, is the huge tomb of Canova, constructed for him after his death in 1822 from a design of his intended for a tomb for Titian. Then on the main entrance wall is a monument on the right of the door to Pietro Bernardo, of date and style and elegance which suggest that it may be by Tullio Lombardo. The plainer monument on the left of the door is 16th century Lombardesque. And over the holy-water stoups by the first columns are figures of 'St Antony' and 'Charity' by Campagna.

First on the right wall of the nave is an elaborate altar designed by Longhena, but with lesser men's sculpture on it. Next is the truly appalling tomb erected in the mid 19th century for Titian in place of Canova's. After this the first monument to note is the third along from Titian's, called the Zane altar, with statues on it by Vittoria of 'St Jerome' in the centre and an apostle at either end.

Next to note are those in the right transept, that on the right wall being a monument to Jacopo Marcello, who was killed in 1484 (fighting the Turks at Gallipoli), with his armed figure on top and three overburdened figures at the bottom purporting to carry the whole affair. This may well be by Pietro Lombardo. On the end wall on the right is a florid Gothic monument to the Beato Pacifico, by tradition the founder of the church. It is Florentine and early 15th century. Next to it, over the door, is a monument to Benedetto Pesaro, who died in 1603, with a statue of him by Lorenzo Bregno. At this point, as we are at the sacristy door, you should see the lunette in the cloister which leads off it of the 'Virgin and Child with St Francis and Elizabeth presenting Doge Dandolo and his Dogaressa', by Paolo Veneziano. Also it is just worth mentioning that the carved wooden clock-frame on the left wall as you face Bellini's triptych, and close to it, is by the same Pianta whose carvings are in the Scuola di S. Rocco. The tiny 'Hagar' above it is by Pittoni.

Back in the church, the next monument, high up on the left of the sacristy door, is that of Paolo Savelli and is the earliest (*c.* 1410) equestrian statue in Venice. It stands on a sarcophagus with the figures of the 'Virgin and Child' in the middle, and of the 'Virgin' and the 'Angel of the Annunciation' at either end, ascribed by some to Jacopo della Quercia, by others to a Venetian strongly influenced by Florentine early-Renaissance sculpture.

Then we come to the chapels flanking the chancel, and in the first (along the line from right to left), over the altar, is a good polyptych by Bartolomeo Vivarini, and on the right wall an early 15th century Gothic memorial to two brothers called Bernardo. In the second chapel two early 14th century sarcophagi with recumbent statues on them face one another, that of a Florentine ambassador called Duccio degli Alberti, who died in 1336, on the right, and on the left that of an unknown knight in armour. In the third is Donatello's 'John the Baptist'. In the chancel itself on the right wall is a great monument to Doge Francesco Foscari, mid 15th century, in a style transitional between late Gothic and early Renaissance, attributed first to Bartolomeo Bon, then to Antonio Rizzo and now to Antonio and Paolo Bregno. Opposite it is the most magnificent Renaissance monument in Venice, late 15th century, a memorial to Doge Nicolo Tron by Rizzo.

There is nothing of any importance in the chapel nearest the chancel on the left. In the next one there is on the right wall a tomb, and standing on it an unsuccessful statue of Melchior Trevisan, a great Venetian general, by Lorenzo Bregno. The unpretentious recumbent figure on the left wall, of an unknown warrior, is dishonoured by hundreds of names scrawled all round it. In the next chapel, over the altar, is a handsome painting started by Alvise Vivarini and finished by Marco Basaiti.

Next comes the Corner Chapel, recently given a low angle railing so that you can see its lovely contents. Over the altar is triptych by Bartolomeo Vivarini, of 'St Mark between Saints', and above are the remains of some stained-glass windows. Facing you, in a Mantegnaesque surround, is an early Renaissance tomb with a beautiful figure of an angel on it, anonymous, but one of the supreme works of art of the period when Venice first felt the influence of Florence. And on the font is one of Sansovino's greatest figures in marble, a full-length statue of 'St John the Baptist'.

Lastly in the nave stands the choir, a mixture of styles and periods, Gothic in origin, completed in the early Renaissance manner under Pietro Lombardo and somewhat marred by two pointless 18th century 'cantorie' at either side. There are good figures on it and good reliefs and woodwork, and above, a grand bronze Renaissance crucifix.

(Also in Index of Artists: Bambini, Licinio, Palma Giovane.)

San Gallo   SM 11
The picture over the High Altar has been attributed to Tintoretto, but is by some much less distinguished artist. On the altar on the left is a fine 18th century ivory crucifix.

San Geremia   W Can: 4
Founded at the end of the 13th century but badly damaged by fire in 1848, and almost entirely rebuilt. The campanile is possibly 12th century, the belfry being a later addition. The statues of 'St Peter' and 'St Jeremiah' on the altar are by a late 18th century sculptor called Ferrari, a pupil of Torretti, and in the chapel on the right nearest the chancel is a passable picture of 'The Coronation of Venice by St Magnus, with the Madonna', by Palma Giovane.

The Gesuati (properly Santa Maria del Rosario or dei Gesuati)   ED 4
This 18th century church was rebuilt by the Dominicans and consecrated in 1736. Its rather splendid architecture is purely formal for its period, inside and out. The pictures on the ceiling are by Tiepolo and are well lit besides being well painted and in reasonably good condition. The central one represents the 'Institution of the Rosary' and at the foot of it St Dominic has defeated Heresy and is distributing rosaries to the crowd. Nearer the door is 'St Dominic in Glory'. The picture nearer the High Altar is of 'St Dominic blessing a

Dominican', probably Father Paolo, who took a leading part in building the church. The smaller grisailles on the ceiling are school work. The first picture on the right wall of the nave is one of Tiepolo's noblest works. It represents the Madonna watching over three Dominican saints, St Catherine of Siena, St Rose of Lima, and St Agnes. You may never be happy with Tiepolo as a religious artist, but this is a superb example of his painting. Two along the same wall is a well-painted, slightly faded, quiet and unemotional picture by Piazzetta of three sainted Dominican friars. The 'St Dominic' in between is also by him but is in a deplorable condition.

On the left wall of the nave the picture farthest from the main door is of the 'Crucifixion' and is by Tintoretto, but it has been considerably restored and, nearest the door on this side is 'St Thomas and St Peter Martyr with Pope Pius V' by Sebastiano Ricci. It is an unhappy composition, with five women and three men crowded in confusion at the foot of the Cross.

The Gesuiti (properly Santa Maria Assunta)   E Can: 1
This large early 18th century baroque Jesuit church is decorated inside with a great deal of marble intarsia work calculated to simulate tapestry. Perhaps the most successful features of this are the imitations of a curtain over the pulpit and of a carpet in front of the High Altar. Of the many prominent statues the best are those, at the corners where the nave, chancel and transepts meet, of the four Archangels by Torretti, and two more Archangels by him on either side of the High Altar. The picture of the 'Virgin and Saints' on the third altar on the right is by Balestra. There is a monument by Campagna in the chapel on the left of the chancel, and a badly restored 'Assumption of the Virgin' by Tintoretto in the left transept.

The only great work of art, however, is the picture by Titian over the altar nearest the door on the left of the nave, of the 'Martyrdom of St Laurence', who is being roasted alive. Impossible to see without having the lights turned on (which the sacristan will do), this is an exercise by Titian in dispersed illumination against darkness.

Opposite the church is the Oratorio dei Cruciferi. If you can get into it, you will find it full of pictures by Palma Giovane, painted while he was still strongly influenced by his great teacher, Titian.

(Also in the Index of Artists: Fumiani, Palma Giovane.)

San Giacomo dell'Orio   SC 5

The name is believed to be a corruption of 'del lauro' or 'd'allora', meaning 'of the laurel tree'. It is a very ancient church, founded in the 9th century, but reconstructed in the 13th and unsatifactorily refurbished in he 16th. Fortunately the Gothic wooden roof, of the early 14th century, survives, with some other parts of the first structure.

Just inside the main entrance on the right is an interesting little Greek font. On the organ above the door, and on either side of it, are paintings that have been tentatively ascribed to Andrea Schiavone, but those on the organ, which are hard to see, look too stiff to be his work, and the others too feeble, unless they have been very harshly treated.

The new sacristy, entered from the right transept, has a ceiling picture of the 'Triumph of Faith' and four small 'Fathers of the Church' round it, all said to be by Veronese, but not very important works. Berenson ascribes only three of the Fathers, Laurence, Jerome and Prosper, to him, and not the centre panel.

Over the High Altar is a picture of the 'Virgin and Child with St Andrew, St James, St Cosmas and St Damian', by Lorenzo Lotto, competently designed but said to have been heavily restored. The two marble crosses on either side of the chancel are part of the misguided 16th century restoration of the church, but are fine and tasteful in themselves. Berenson considers the 'Adoration of the Shepherds' in the second chapel to the left of the chancel to be an early Veronese.

(Also in Index of Artists: Palma Giovane.)

San Giacomo di Rialto   R 2

This tiny church was first built in the 5th century, but the present building was started in the 11th and finished in the 12th and so is contemporary with St Mark's. On the opposite side of the small square in which it stands is a low column, like the Pietra del Bando in front of St Mark's, from which proclamations were read, but it is often shut off so that you cannot see it properly. The portico in front of the church, with five columns topped by elaborate capitals, is the only original example of this feature of early Venetian churches. The clock on the façade was constructed early in the 15th century.

Inside, the columns again have rich capitals. The marble statue of 'St James' on the High Altar is by Vittoria, but done in his old age and rather feeble. On the sole altar on the left of the nave the handsome bronze statue of 'St Antony Abbot' is by Campagna.

San Giobbe   W Can: 2

This remote but once important church was designed by Gambello and dates from 1450. Some of the original Gothic structure of this date, such as the brick tower, survives or shows through subsequent restorations, the most far-reaching of which were carried out in classical Renaissance terms by Pietro Lombardo as early as 1470. His are the fine doorway and the lunette and three statues on the facade. Inside, the chancel with its splendid arch, the Choir behind the altar and the two chapels on either side of it are all by him or, under his influence, by some of the army of assistants that he used.

At the end of the right wall, beyond a picture by Paris Bordone of 'St Peter, St Andrew and St Nicholas', is a chapel leading to the sacristy, which belongs to Gambello's first building. On its altar is a pleasant painting of 'The Nativity' by Savoldo. In the sacristy, behind an ancient wrought-iron gate, is a triptych by Antonio Vivarini. The chancel has lovely carvings by Lombardo. In the chapel on the left of it the admirable statue of 'St Francis' is by Lorenzo Bregno, and so also is that of 'St Luke' in the Renaissance chapel nearest the entrance door on the left of the nave. The chapel next to this is entirely Florentine in its decoration, much of which, including the small statue of 'St John the Baptist', is by Antonio Rossellino, while the roof is Della Robbia.

San Giorgio dei Greci   W Cas: 10

The church, belonging to the Greek Orthodox community, is the centre of a happy group of buildings that span one hundred and forty years. It was itself designed by two Lombard architects and built between 1539 and 1561, and its dome (which is not, as some say, by Palladio) was added in 1571. It consists of a single nave, with a handsomely railed monks' gallery (barco) over the door, wooden stalls along the sides, a screen (iconostasis), gilt and painted right up to the ceiling, in front of the chancel or 'hieron' and two gated apses, of which that on the left contains a fine 12th century icon of the Virgin, now darkened with age and hung high up on the left wall, where it is hard to see.

The campanile, which now leans considerably, was added at the end of the 16th century, and in the second half of the 17th century Longhena added the Scuoletta and Collegio on

22   San Giobbe. The 'Nativity' by Savoldo

23 San Giorgio Maggiore

the other side of the church, and the wall along the canal.

At the adjoining Ponte dei Greci stands (north-east of the bridge) the old Palazzo Zorzi, 15th century Gothic, tattered but still noble. You are also close to the Palazzo Priuli, *q.v.* under S. Zaccaria.

San Giorgio Maggiore

(Vaporetti on the 'Circolare' run, which serves S. Giorgio, go every fifteen minutes from the landing stage well east of the Doge's Palace now called S. Zaccaria—S. Marco.)

This is one of the few churches by Palladio in Venice. It was started in 1566 and finished, after his death, in 1610. The facade is one of his great achievements. On it are busts of two doges, and no one knows why they have their hats on back to front.

Inside, round the door, too high up to be seen clearly, are statues of the four Evangelists by Vittoria. On the right of the nave there is a very dark 'Adoration of the Shepherds' by Jacopo Bassano over the first altar and over the second a gaunt and, to my mind, unholy wooden carving of Christ on the Cross. Then comes a poor picture of mixed martyrdoms from the school of Tintoretto. In the right transept are two fine 18th century bronze candelabra, and in the chapel on the right of the chancel the 'Madonna and Saints' by Sebastiano Ricci, one of his first pictures and therefore a novelty in its time as a herald of Venetian 18th century revulsion against the heaviness of the 17th century. Its main influence is Veronese, with a touch of Jacopo Bassano in the kneeling figure of St Paul, and the critic Longhi sees Correggio in it as well. In front of the High Altar on the balustrade are two more fine candelabra, by Nicolò Roccatagliata. On the High Altar itself is a grand group of the four Evangelists supporting a globe on which stands the figure of God the Father with a triangular halo, by Campagna, made in 1591–3.

On either side are two important pictures by Tintoretto, the 'Last Supper' and the 'Fall of Manna', the gift of manna being regarded as an act of God foreshadowing the gift of the Eucharist, and both pictures being visible to communicants at the altar rail. They were painted in 1594,* the year in which Tintoretto died, and show his imagination as vivid as ever. In

*Lorenzetti says that they were finished by 1591, but I have followed Berenson and others.

the 'Fall of Manna' he has depicted men and women occupied, so as to exercise his skill at figure-drawing, in a landscape of his choice, without, that is, making any special statement about the subject. In the 'Last Supper' he has rejoiced in the *tour de force* of the smoke swirling into a cloud of angels and in the dramatic play of light from various sources including the 'gloria' round the head of Christ.

Behind the altar in the choir are elaborate choir-stalls in carved wood, the work of a Flemish artist, Albert van der Brulle, and a Venetian, G. Gatti, in collaboration (1594-8). In front are bronze statues of 'St George' and 'St Stephen' by Nicolò Roccatagliata. Through the door on the right before you go into the choir, and then immediately to the right and up a circular stone stairway, is a chapel (Cappella Superiore) in which is a picture of 'St George and the Dragon' by Carpaccio, very like that in the Schiavoni, but with a deep landscape background. It has a dull finish, being painted in tempera, and it is useless to try to see it without having the light turned on. The switch, in case the sacristan is not with you, is on the left wall (as you stand facing the picture), high up where the panelling begins.

Back in the main church, the picture over the altar in the left transept, of the 'Martyrdom of St Stephen', was quite highly praised by Ruskin, who believed it to be by Tintoretto, but it is now thought to be a studio picture painted by his pupils or perhaps by his son.

The Campanile, in which there is a lift, gives a splendid view of Venice and its waterways and islands. A visit at sunset is strongly recommended.

The other buildings on the island, which are open only on special occasions, are exquisite, especially the first cloisters, by Palladio or Scamozzi, the double entrance, of Egyptian grandeur, to the refectory, which Palladio finished from an earlier design, and Longhena's main staircase. They have all been most worthily restored by the Giorgio Cini Foundation.

(Also in Index of Artists: Palma Giovane.)

Scuola di San Giorgio degli Schiavoni   W Cas: 13

This small building was originally a hotel built by Dalmatian merchants for Dalmatian sailors—'Schiavoni' being Italian for Dalmatians (or Slavs)—in the 15th century. It was consecrated to two saints, George and Tryphonius, particularly revered in Dalmatia. The marvellous pictures in it by

Carpaccio, painted between 1502 and 1508, show the legend of St George and the Dragon in three scenes, and in one the main incident in the legend of St Tryphonius, the others being the 'Agony in the Garden' and the 'Calling of St Matthew', and three of St Jerome.

Starting on the left, the first three are of St George wounding the dragon, his arrival in the city leading it (which is in the legend) and then the baptism by him of the father and mother of the princess.

The first picture is one of the most ingratiating in the world, in spite of the remains of the dragon's victims, which are indeed gruesome. St George and his horse are magnificent, and every detail, both in the background and more particularly in the foreground, is painted beautifully. Ruskin singled out the snake just left of centre near the lower edge, which, he says, Carpaccio with a few strokes of his brush, in three minutes at most, has made black, slimy, springy and close down on the earth.

In the second picture St George is rather stiff and the dragon is, not unnaturally, thoroughly depressed. The heads of the princess and her father and their head-dresses caught Ruskin's eye. He called them quite perfect and added that 'there is nothing elsewhere in art that is the like of this little piece of work for supreme, serene, unassuming, unfaltering sweetness of painter's perfect art'. There is also a typical sureness of eye in the painting of St George's horse, pawing the ground as a horse would in the circumstances.

The third picture, of the baptism of the princess's father, has a fine band with trumpets and shawms, a fine red parrot and a very bored dog. St George, as Ruskin pointed out, is holding his mantle back in the most natural possible way, because the water is bound to splash.

Next is the episode of St Tryphonius, which requires some explaining. As a boy he cured an emperor's daughter of a devil, which he put into the form of a tame basilisk. Or else he simply tamed a basilisk which had been giving trouble, and led it about the court. An untamed basilisk killed people with its glance, but there is no question of this happening here, and Carpaccio has made it a comic heraldic beast. The group in the loggia on the left is, so Ruskin says, 'a picture in itself, far more lovely as a composition than the finest Titian or Veronese, simple and pleasant as the summer air and lucent as a morning cloud'.

The 'Agony in the Garden' is a picture of somewhat the same kind as the two representations of the subject by Giovanni Bellini and Mantegna, both of which Carpaccio could perhaps have seen, and which are now in the National Gallery in London.

'The Calling of St Matthew' is described by Ruskin as 'a lovely picture in every sense and power of painting, natural and graceful and quiet and pathetic, divinely religious, yet as decorative and dainty as a bank of violets in spring'. The background is pure Venetian.

'St Jerome and the Lion' shows Carpaccio's habit of portraying an episode just as it comes to him, in this case as a comic one. It is said that the drawing of the running monks was exquisitely naturalistic but is lost under their robes.

In the 'Death of St Jerome' the monks are again ridiculous, bu the Saint himself is dignified and beneficent, as he is in the previous picture. Ruskin calls attention to the beautiful little scroll bearing Carpaccio's signature, held in its mouth by a tiny lizard. The building with a balcony in the middle distance on the left is a model of his perfection in depicting substance and light with equal truthfulness.

The last picture may be of St Jerome in his study, perhaps when he was secretary to Pope Damasus (in A.D. 382), or Carpaccio's idea of the Saint in heaven, but most probably it represents St Augustine, who by legend was writing to St Jerome at the moment of the latter's death and saw a sudden light from heaven to warn him of it (Plate 24). It is marvellous in composition and in colour and detail. One of the scrolls on the floor is a long passage of melody, which is the music for a hymn to St Augustine. 'It is quite impossible,' says Ruskin, 'to find more right and beautiful painting of detail, or more truthful tones of atmosphere and shadow affecting interior colours.'

(Also in Index of Artists: Palma Giovane.)

San Giovanni in Bragora   **W Cas: 16**
S. Giovanni is St John the Baptist, to whom the church is dedicated, and no one knows what 'in Bragora' means. Though the building has been partly spoiled by renovations, the pleasant simple façade, dating from the second half of the 15th century, has been spared from them and is of a traditional Venetian-Byzantine design.

Inside, the renovations have confused the architecture and basic decoration. There is, however, one superb picture, Cima

24 San Giorgio degli Schiavoni. 'St Augustine' by Carpaccio

da Conegliano's 'Baptism of Christ', over the High Altar. The background is worth lingering over, after the beauty of the design and the figures is absorbed, even though the picture is hung so high that it is not too easy to see. Burckhardt's opinion was that 'in the dignity of the head of Christ, in the beauty of the Angels, and the solemn gestures of the Baptist, this picture is incomparable'.

There is another smaller picture by Cima, of 'St Helena and Constantine on either side of the Cross'. This is often moved, but in 1975 was in the right nave, and balancing it on the other side of the door was another much-moved picture, the 'Risen Christ' by Alvise Vivarini, which is interesting for being the first break by this traditional painter with his traditions, there being in it some of the freedom of his greater contemporaries. In the chapel nearest the chancel, on the left of the nave, is the most vulgar picture in Venice, painted in 1925 in the manner of Piazzetta, of 'St Theresa' kneeling before an angel seated immodestly on a table. Nearer the door on the same side of the nave is a reverent picture of the 'Madonna' by Alvise Vivarini and next to it, unless it has been moved again, is a triptych by his uncle Bartolomeo of the 'Virgin between St John the Baptist and St Andrew'.

(Also in Index of Artists: Bissolo, Bordone, Marieschi, Palma Giovane.)

25   San Giovanni in Bragora. The 'Baptism of Christ' by Cima da Conegliano

San Giovanni Crisostomo R 3

This church was built about 1500. The architect was Coducci and the facade is simple but elegant. Inside it is dark and gives an un-spacious impression, partly because it is indeed not very large and partly because there is nearly always something going on in it. It contains a superb late picture by Giovanni Bellini, of St Jerome in the centre reading a book propped on a conveniently shaped tree, with St Christopher and St Augustine on either side in the foreground. It is badly placed in a dark little chapel on the right of the nave. There are some weak lights for it and it is worth having them turned on and waiting until one's eyes get used to the dimness in order to see the marvellous detail of the picture. The infant Christ on St Christopher's shoulder is enchanting. There is a slight flavour of Giorgione in the style. Ruskin thought it one of the best pictures in the world.

Behind the High Altar is a good picture (1509-11) by Sebastiano del Piombo, painted in his Giorgionesque style. It is of 'St John Chrysostom and St John the Baptist, St Liberale, St Mary Magdalene, St Agnes and St Catherine'. And over the second altar on the left of the nave is a bas-relief by Tullio Lombardo of the 'Coronation of the Virgin', a noble work in strictly classical style, but decidedly stiff.

(Also in Index of Artists: Mansueti.)

San Giovanni Decollato (called S. Zan Degola) SC 6

The columns are 11th century. The frescoes round the church are 15th century, but only fragments of them remain. The roof is 'carena di nave', painted.

San Giovanni Elemosinario R 1

The present church, which is tucked away behind part of the Rialto market, may have been designed by Scarpagnino and was finished in 1529. In it are two moderate but large pictures by Leonardo Corona, 'Christ Raised on the Cross', on the right entrance wall, and 'The Fall of Manna' on the left. In the chapel on the right of the chancel is 'St Roch, St Sebastian and St Catherine' by Pordenone. The principal treasure is 'St John distributing Alms' by Titian over the High Altar, very poorly lit (as is the rest of the church), but well cleaned fairly recently. It is a simple painting of great dignity.

Over it is yet a third picture by Corona, of the 'Resurrection' In the sacristy is the 'Virgin with St Philip' by Pittonio.

(Also in Index of Artists: Palma Giovane, Marieschi, Domenico Tintoretto.)

Scuola di San Giovanni Evangelista SP 1

The school was a seminary for flagellant Franciscan friars and was subscribed to generously by the people of Venice because of the help that the friars gave to the sick and the help that they were believed to give to all by their holy works in times of epidemics or plagues. It is a very beautiful example of Venetian Renaissance architecture. The façade of the school itself was built in 1434, and the rest was added during the next sixty years. The external screen (1481, perhaps designed by Pietro Lombardo) and the courtyard are delightful. If you ring and wait, the custodian will eventually open the door and admit you to two plain but handsome downstairs rooms, an overdecorated upstairs room and a very fine double staircase by Mauro Coducci between them. In the lovely late 15th century double window at the top of the staircase are two tiny pieces of old stained glass. The main upper hall has pictures on the wall by Domenico Tintoretto (first and fourth) and Sante Peranda (second), and others, less dull, on the ceiling by Marieschi and Guarana, as noted in the Index of Artists, round the central panel of the 'Overthrow of Antichrist' by Piazzetta's pupil, Giuseppe Angeli.

The Hall of the Cross leads off this upper hall. The pictures painted for it are now in *Room XX* of the Accademia, but the Relic of the Cross which is the subject of the pictures is in the reliquary on the altar. And beside the altar is the 15th century gilt wooden staff on which it was carried.

(Also in Index of Artists: Palma Giovane, Domenico Tiepolo, Domenico Tintoretto.)

Santi Giovanni e Paolo W Cas: 3

This enormous brick church was built for the Dominicans over a period of two centuries and was finally consecrated in 1430. Outside it is the famous bronze statue of Bartolomeo Colleoni which was designed and mostly made by Verrocchio, and then finished and cast by Leopardi (Plate 28). It is of tremendous power, and no doubt the finest equestrian statue in the world. Colleoni was one of the condottieri

26 San Giovanni Crisostomo. 'St Jerome, St Christopher and St Augustine' by Giovanni Bellini

(mercenaries with private armies) who as a rule fought for whichever state paid them best. He was not the greatest of them, but endeared himself to the Venetians by fighting only for them, not changing sides like the others. He left all his money to Venice on condition that a statue of him was put in front of St Mark's. The Venetians took the money and put this statue not in front of the Basilca di San Marco but here façade of which forms the north side of this piazza.

The magnificent main portal of the church was added in the second half of the 15th century. It is in the style of that era, a blend of Venetian-Gothic and early Renaissance. There is no record to tell us whose work it was, and its ascription to Antonio Gambello is no more than a conjecture based on his being a leading architect of that time.

Inside, the entrance wall is virtually covered by three memorials, each of one of the Mocenigo doges. That on the left as you face the wall is the most admired. It is by Pietro Lombardo and is typically noble and severe. That on the right is by Tullio Lombardo, and that in the centre has two of Pietro Lombardo's figures, made apparently for the one by him on the left.

On the right wall is a polyptych the attribution of which has been disputed for three centuries but which is now generally accepted as an early work of Giovanni Bellini, though the predella may be by someone else. Above is a Pietà and below St Vincent between St Christopher and St Sebastian. The predella pictures are of the life of St Vincent. Beyond, in the last chapel before the right transept, is a ceiling by Piazzetta, greatly admired and probably once superb, but in a poor state until its heavy restoration, with much repainting, in 1969. To be fair, it may well now look much as it originally did, and the figures of God the Father and Our Lord above the Virgin, all in white, are beautifully contrasted with the warm brown and blue of the rest. The subject is the 'Apotheosis of St Dominic' and friars of that Order are contemplating the scene from below the prostrate saint.

In the right transept is one of the very few good stained-glass windows in Italy, based mostly on designs by Bartolomeo Vivarini and made at Murano in the 15th century.* Below, on the right of the door, is an excellent

*On high is God the Father, then comes the Annunciation flanked by two prophets. Then the Virgin and St John the Baptist between St Paul and St Peter. Then the Evangelists and some Fathers of the Church, then four Dominican saints, and lastly St George and St Theodore, killing their dragons, outside the sainted soldiers, John and Paul, after whom the church is named.

San Giovanni
Evangelista

picture of 'St Antonino distributing Alms' by Lorenzo Lotto, and on the left a very good one by Rocco Marconi of 'Christ, St Peter and St Andrew' with traces of the influences of Bellini and Giorgione. They are hard to see unless you pay to put the lights on. On the right-hand wall is a picture of 'Christ carrying the Cross', by Alvise Vivarini, recently cleaned, but in a pitiable state, and, alas, awkward and positively ugly.

In the chancel the two monuments on the left are notable. The further one is either by the Lombardi or perhaps by Leopardi, but the statues on it of St Catherine and St Mary Magdalene are by Lorenzo Bregno and are out of scale. On the nearer one, which is not complete, the Madonna and two angels are 14th century, Tuscan, and quite possibly by Nino Pisano. In the second chapel on the left of the chancel is a sarcophagus (on the right wall) by Paolo delle Masegne, with

28 Santi Giovanni e Paolo (outside) 'Bartolomeo Colleoni'
by Verrocchio

an imposing armed figure lying on it.

In the Cappella del Rosario, entered at the end of the left transept, there are three ceiling paintings of first quality by Paolo Veronese, the 'Annunciation', the 'Assumption' and the 'Adoration of the Shepherds'. The picture on the left as you enter (moved hither from the first chapel on the left of the chancel), another version of 'Adoration of the Shepherds', is ascribed by some to Veronese and looks as if the lovely figures and the lower part must be by him but the less important upper part may have been painted by a pupil. The two bronze candelabra in the chancel are by Vittoria.

Back into the main church, on the left wall of the nave, when you have passed the sacristy door, first comes a monument to Doge Pasquale Malipiero by Pietro Lombardo, a refined Renaissance work of about 1470, and next to it, high up, another monument, fifty years later, with nothing to commend it except the recumbent figure of the senator whose memorial it is. Underneath are two arched niches. That on the right has an elegant 14th century front to its sarcophagus and that on the left, which is about 1550 and is the monument of Alvise Trevisan, has behind him, on either side of a rather unattractive putto, piles of books to show that he was a man of letters. Next is an early 17th century wooden equestrian statue of a condottiere, and then the elegant 15th century tomb of Doge Tommaso Mocenigo, mostly by Pietro Lamberti with strong Florentine influence, including on the left edge a figure taken from Donatello's St George.

A fine classic monument by Pietro Lombardo follows, and, after that, a poor 17th century copy of one of Titian's great masterpieces, 'The Death of St Peter Martyr', which was destroyed by fire, along with pictures by Bellini and Tintoretto and others once in this church, in 1867.* This is followed by a florid 17th century equestrian statue, and then, after a 19th century monument, a fine altar by Guglielmo dei Grigi, made in 1524, with a poor picture in it, but on it one of Vittoria's best statues, of St Jerome.

(Also in Index of Artists: Palma Giovane, Bartolomeo Vivarini, Campagna, Scamozzi, Vittoria.)

*There is an excellent small version by Alfred Stevens in a private collection in London.

San Giuseppe di Castello   E Cas: 5

In the atrium under the barco (ruined by a cheap modern front) are fragments, five on each side, of naïve but interesting wooden carvings, impossible to date. The first picture on the right of the nave, 'St Michael fighting the Devil, and an Observer', is attributed to Tintoretto. It is in a poor state, with much bad repainting, and may be a school picture, but Berenson describes it as a late picture by Tintoretto himself. The 'Adoration of the Shepherds' over the High Altar is too muddled in design and unsubtle in colour to be by Veronese. The fine bust of a Procurator called Grimani on the left wall of the chancel is by Vittoria. On the large monument on the left wall of the nave the clumsy marble statues (only the 'Virgin and Child', high up, is of any merit) and the bronze bas-reliefs, which are much better, are by Campagna.

Palazzo Labia   W Can: 4

After years of private ownership in which no one was admitted, permission can now be obtained to see the main hall. In it are magnificent frescoes by Tiepolo of Antony and Cleopatra, repaired and slightly faded, but still recognizable as masterpieces. On the is the 'Banquet', with 'Time carrying off Beauty' above it, and on the left the 'Embarkation'. In the centre of the ceiling is 'Poetry on a Winged Horse', as brilliant a feat of design as those of the ceiling pictures of Veronese, whose influence is visble throughout the room.

Tiepolo owes the architectural designs in which his frescoes are fitted to G. M. Colonna, but he has himself taken advantage of every opportunity of placing smaller figures and groups.

San Lazzaro dei Mendicanti   W Cas: 1

Early 17th century, designed perhaps by Scamozzi except for the facade, which is by an imitator of Palladio. Inside there is a huge screen by Sardi, built as a memorial to Alvise Mocenigo, who beat the Turks in Crete in the 1650s. The top part of it, on the side that you look back on after you have passed through it, has a fine figure of the hero in the centre, and at the sides is alive with martial glory.

The first picture on the right wall, of the 'Crucifixion, with St Mary and St John', which has been heavily restored, is ascribed to Paolo Veronese by some, but not by Berenson. On the left wall the first picture as you come back from the chancel has also been damaged and badly restored but is of some interest as it is the only one by Guercino in Venice. The next one, of 'St Ursula and the 11,000 Virgins', is by Tintoretto. It is good and well preserved, and it would be better known if it were not in this church of 'St Lazarus of the Beggars', which is nearly always closed, being, so it seems, virtually a chapel for the hospital which surrounds it.

San Lio   R 7

S. Lio is the Venetian name for the sainted Pope Leo IX who was a friend to Venice. Over the first altar on the left, as you enter, is a painting of 'St James of Compostella' by Titian. It is sadly in need of cleaning and perhaps of some repair, but when illuminated (and the sacristan will turn on the light) it can be seen to be a competent and powerful picture. In the chapel on the right of the chancel the decoration is by Pietro and Tullio Lombardo, the 'Pietà with Saints' over the altar being by the latter, and the four 'Evangelists' round the cupola probably by the former. The 'Dead Christ' over the High Altar is by Palma Giovane. On the ceiling of the nave are paintings, some in monochrome, by Domenico Tiepolo.

A short distance along the street that leads from the little campo westwards towards the Rialto is the Ponte S. Antonio. The third building down on the left on the S. Lio side is the Palazzo Gussoni, late 15th century, adapted from an older Gothic building by Pietro Lombardo, who kept the original six round-arched windows in the first storey.

San Luca   SM 2

Over the High Altar is the 'Virgin appering to St Luke', a worn picture by Veronese in which the figure of the saint must once have been impressive. His bull looks very tame. It is hard to understand why the Virgin and Child are repeated in the lower left-hand corner. In the chapel to the right is a picture of the 'Virgin in Glory and Saints' by Palma Giovane.

On the right-hand altar on the left is a small 15th century marble statuette of St Catherine, a gentle ingenuous thing by an unidentified sculptor of the Lombardesque school, possibly Rizzo.

The Madonna dell'Orto (or Sta. Maria dell'Orto)   W Can: 6

This church is a very noble and beautiful example of Venetian Gothic architecture and, as it is also full of fine things, it is well worth the rather long walk required to reach it. It was first built in the middle of the 14th century and was then dedicated to St Christopher, whose statue is above the main doorway. It was almost completely reconstructed in the 15th century, and the facade decorated with sculpture, including this statue and those of the 'Virgin' and the 'Angel of the Annunciation' on either side over the doorway.

The new façade was set up early in the century, the side windows were added later, and later still, about 1450, the doorway, with its Renaissance side pillars, and the twelve Apostles in the niches over the wings. The rest of the building was not completed until near the end of the century. At some stage the church was renamed in honour of a statue of the Madonna which was found in a nearby orchard (orto) about 1370 and was believed to have fallen from heaven.

Inside, first of all on the right, almost in the corner, is a vigorous but not very ingratiating half-length carving of the 'Madonna and Child' by a contemporary of Rizzo and therefore late 15th century. On the right wall first comes a superb picture by Cima da Conegliano, of 'St John the Baptist between four Saints', recently cleaned, full of light and one of Cima's greatest achievements. The ruined pergola frames and unites the group. The glow of the background sky and all the light on all the flesh, fabrics, stone and leaves go beyond Ruskin's 'deep remembrance of reality', and are true descriptions in colour of real things seen in real light. The other Saints, St Paul, St Jerome, St Mark and St Peter, in red, blue and green robes, leave the Baptist dominant in his plain brown habit. The bird on top of the pergola is hard to see, but is undoubtedly a little owl, and Ruskin gives as examples of 'loving fidelity to the thing studied' the oak and the fig in this picture, the Erba della Madonna on the wall, the ivy and other creepers, and a strawberry plant in the foreground with one berry just set, another half ripe and a third quite ripe, 'all patiently and innocently painted from the real thing, and therefore most divine'.

Much further along over the sacristy door is Tintoretto's famous 'Presentation of the Virgin', in which drama is created by the beggars leaning forward in the shadow on the left, and serenity, in contrast, by the figure of the Child with the halo relieved, by way of a marvellous tour de force, against the lightest part of the sky. It was painted in the 1550s, about eighteen years after Titian's similar picture in Room XXII of the Accademia. In the sacristy is the stone figure of the Madonna referred to above, which is 14th century and freely restored.

Tintoretto, his wife and eight other members of his family lie buried beneath the pavement of the chapel on the right of the chancel. On either side of the chancel itself are two huge early masterpieces by him, the 'Last Judgement' and 'The Worship of the Golden Calf'. These pictures and the 'Presentation' started Ruskin on his worship of Tintoretto. They are brilliant achievements, though it is possible to admire them without liking them. In the 'Last Judgement' Ruskin confidently identified the rushing river as 'the oceans of the earth and the waters of the firmament gathered into one white ghastly cataract; the river of the wrath of God, roaring down into the gulf where the world has melted with its fervent heat, choked with the ruins of nations . . .' In 'the Golden Calf' one of the principal figures bearing the letter on which the image is carried is said to be a self-portrait of Tintoretto and, if so, it must be the man in front on the right with his chest bared. The woman in blue is said to be a portrait of his wife. Behind the altar are two pictures by him, once organ doors, the 'Martyrdom of St Paul' on the right, and on the left, its luminosity and liveliness revealed by recent cleaning, 'The Miraculous Apparition of the Cross to St Peter'. They flank a weak altar-piece by Palma Giovane, and above, also by Tintoretto, are 'Temperance', 'Justice', 'Prudence' and 'Fortitude'.

30 The Madonna dell'Orto. 'St John the Baptist and Saints' by Cima
da Conegliano

In the recessed chapel in the centre of the left wall of the nave are six busts of members of the Contarini family, the two in the centre being by Vittoria. Also, over the altar, is yet another early Tintoretto, 'St Agnes restoring the Son of a Roman Prefect to Life'. This makes ten pictures by him in this church, which was his parish church and in which he chose to be buried. In the last chapel as you come back to the door on this side is a charming 'Madonna and Child' by Giovanni Bellini, the Baby's hair being specially pretty.

The church was restored and repaired by the British flood relief fund in 1969. The handsome 15th century cloisters, of brick arches on stone columns, were rescued and repaired also, after years of neglect.

(Also in Index of Artists: Palma Vecchio, Domenico Tintoretto, Sardi.)

Pinacoteca Manfrediana ED 8

This small gallery is in the Seminario Patriarcale, next to the Salute, on its left as you look at it from the Canal. It is said to be open at times during school terms of the Seminario. During the school holidays it is impossible to get into the gallery without an introduction from the 'Belle Arti' or some other influential source.

When you enter the seminary you come first into the cloisters, which have ancient Roman stelae and other stonework in them, the best exhibit being a robed statue on the left side looking into the court, by Vittoria. The staircase which leads up to the loggia, library, refectory and picture gallery was designed by Longhena, and on its ceiling is a large and robust painting of the 'Apotheosis of St Jerome' by Zanchi.

At the top of the stairs turn right along the loggia, and on the left is a well-made early 16th century lavabo with pretty statuettes of St Catherine and St Cecilia on either side. At the end is the entrance to the refectory. Over its door inside the atrium is a made-up lunette of which the 'Virgin and Child' in the centre is probably 15th century. The picture on the left wall within is a 'Crucifixion' by Palma Giovane, in which the figures of Christ and of St Catherine are markedly better than the rest. Farther along the loggia is a picture by Fontebasso on which similarly two figures only are well painted, those of St Francis and of the mother of the child whose blindness he is curing.

In the short passage which leads to a window on the canal there are two competent low-relief marble plaques of ships. Back nearly to the top of the staircase the entrance to the gallery is on the right, and in the little hall outside it are a pretty little 14th century relief of an angel with a lute, coarse high-relief figures of St Matthew in the centre and St Peter and St Mark, and on the wall to the left a 'Nativity' of the period of Pietro Lombardo, and two Greek busts. The relief of St Andrew on the entrance wall is 14th century.

The gallery itself contains an intriguing picture of 'Apollo and Daphne', once the front panel of a cassone, which Berenson ascribes to Giorgione, Baedeker's comment being simply, 'not Giorgione'. It has also been ascribed to Titian, perhaps the ascription now most generally accepted, though it could be Paris Bordone or Andrea Schiavone. This is in the second room, and it is mentioned first because it is the most important work of art in the gallery. In the first room there is a 'Holy Family with an Angel', which once was ascribed to Leonardo da Vinci but now is thought to be the work of a pupil, perhaps from his design. Also there is a 'Virgin and Child' by Cima da Conegliano, and a pair of small doors exquisitiely painted with 'Christ and the Woman of Samaria' and 'Christ appearing to Mary Magdalene' by Filippino Lippi.

The second room contains, besides the 'Apollo and Daphne', a disappointing fresco by Paolo Veronese, and five busts by Vittoria, three of them splendid. In the third room there is a most spirited early terracotta bust of G. M. Amadei by Canova, also two dull ones of cardinals by Bernini.

In the library are three ceiling pictures, the 'Burning of Heretical Books' by Zanchi, the 'Triumph of the Sciences' by Ricci and 'Tutus Livius receiving a Wreath from Minerva' by Bambini, a sparkling trio.

Scuola di San Marco W Cas: 2

This building is nowhere near St Mark's but is in the Campo SS. Giovanni e Paolo, at right angles to the church. It is one of the most striking and elaborate examples of the earliest Venetian-Renaissance architecture. Ruskin more or less accepted this style because of its high-class workmanship and the features, such as round arches, simple shafts and inlaid marble, which it borrowed from the city's 12th century Gothic. And he called the Scuola and the Miracoli 'the two most refined buildings in this style in Venice'.

Not everyone likes the well-known façade which you see

from the Colleoni statue, but it has first-rate credentials. The lower part, with its *trompe l'oeil* decorations, lions and all, is by Pietro Lombardo and his sons, while the top storey is by Mauro Coducci, who took over in 1490 when the Lombardi quarrelled with the fraternity which was employing them. The figure of 'Charity' over the main door is by Bartolomeo Bon or Pietro Lamberti.

Much of the rest of the building was planned later by Sansovino. It is now the city's main hospital and it is not easy for sightseers to get into the rooms upstairs, the library, which was once the 'Salone' for conferences, and the hall that leads off it. In the former is a very rich gilt ceiling and on the right a formal kind of altar by Sansovino framing a rather faded 'Apotheosis of St Mark' by Domenico Tintoretto, with a well designed 'Theft of the Body of St Mark' on the right and a poor faded 'Arrival of the Body of St Mark at Venice' on the left, both also by Him. His too is the central picture opposite of an 'Episode in the Life of St Mark'. On the wall facing the window is a 'Crucifixion' by Donato Veneziano, the only major work in Venice by this 'post-primitive' painter.

In the hall the picture on the entrace wall, the 'Death of St Mark' by a follower of the Bellinis, and those on the left wall of 'Episodes in the St Mark' by Mansueti, hark back to Gentile Bellini and Carpaccio. The picture on the end wall of another 'Episode', this time at sea, may have had some merit when painted by Palma Vecchio, but has been ruined by later overpainting.

San Marcuola (the name is, almost unbelievably, a corruption of SS. Ermagora and Fortunato) W Can: 7

On the left in the chancel is the 'Last Supper', an early version by Tintoretto. On the right wall of the nave, next to the pulpit, is s strange lIttle picture of the Infant Christ with St Andrew and St Catherine on either side. It is heavily restored, was thought to be by Titian, but is now ascribed to his school.

(Also in Index of Artists: Bambini.)

Santa Maria del Carmelo WD 4

This church, known commonly as I Carmini, was built for the Carmelite Order in the 14th century. The façade dates from the beginning of the 16th century and is a plain and handsome example of early Venetian-Renaissance architecture, with contemporary statues on top. The side door goes back to the date of the original building and has on the portico a Venetian-Byzantine design of palm leaves.

Inside, the architecture is the original 14th century Gothic, except for the chancel end, which was redecorated at the beginning of the 16th century in Renaissance style, and the carved woodwork over the middle of the nave, which is 17th century.

On the main entrance wall is a large monument with trophies just above eye level and below them attractive simple representations of sea-battles, warships in fact approaching one another. On the right wall of the nave, over the second altar, is a fine, late, very attractive picture by Cima da Conegliano, representing the worship of the Infant Christ by the Virgin Mary and St Joseph, with Tobias and his guardian angel on the right, St Helena and St Catherine on the left, and a shepherd on his knee with St Joseph's hand on his head and a shepherd boy behind him. A little farther along is a small chapel with most charming bronze angels by Campagna on the railing, a fairly pretty ceiling decoration by Sebastiano Ricci, and a competent statue (dated 1721) of 'Virginity', by Antonio Corradini, on the left. 'The Circumcision', beyond the sacristy door, was once attributed to Tintoretto or Schiavone, but now has been relegated to a very minor artist. Farther on is a beautiful and unusual bronze bas-relief of the 'Deposition', in the style of Donatello, with portraits of Federico Montefeltro and his wife and son, usually now ascribed to Francesco di Giorgio of Siena.

In front of the High Altar are, on either side, an organ loft and a choir gallery. The inner and underneath surfaces are decorated with fine paintings,* all by Andrea Schiavone, except one, of 'God the Father', under the choir gallery, which is less well painted, and later, by Marco Vicentino. On the left wall of the nave, just before the side door as you come from the High Altar, is a first-class and most engaging picture by Lorenzo Lotto of 'St Nicholas [Santa Claus] in Glory' (Plate 31B). Beneath him is one of the best landscapes of the early 16th century, with St George killing the dragon as an incidental part of it.

*The lighting is so bad that those on the outside are invisible. On the inside of the choir gallery are the 'Annunciation' and the 'Adoration of the Shepherds'. The 'Adoration of the Magi' and the 'Circumcision' are on the inside of the organ loft, and on its underside is 'Christ in Glory'.

As you come out of the front door, the undistinguished building on the right at the corner of the canal is known as Othello's house, though it is 19th century and the 14th century building that it replaces, and which was owned by Cristoforo Moro, was pulled down in the 1840s. On the canal side of it is a charming 15th century statue of a page with a shield. Along the Fondamenta del Soccorso, which leads to the left on this side of the canal, is the stately late 17th century Palazzo Zenobio. It is now an Armenian college, and usually you are welcome to go inside, where there is a courtyard with a pretty 18th century loggia and upstairs a spectacular ballroom decorated by an 18th century Frenchman called Louis Daubigny.

Scuola di Santa Maria del Carmine   WD 5

This was built in the 17th century and was perhaps designed by Longhena. On the ground floor there is nothing of interest. The staircase has some attractive stucco decoration. On the ceiling of the main room on the first floor are magnificent pictures by Tiepolo, the large central one being of 'St Simon Stock receiving the Scapular from the Virgin'. In fact the scapular is being proffered to the kneeling saint by an angel below the shimmering Virgin, who is holding Her Child. The picture was painted between 1740 and 1744, and therefore is a work of Tiepolo's maturity. It is marvellously greater than the S. Alvise pictures which were painted not long before, and the reason is that the subject, the luminous sky with a grand apparition shining in it, was his true métier. It was an immediate success, and could well be reckoned his best picture in Venice.

A scapular can mean a shoulder cloak, but for the Carmelite Order it is, as represented here, a loop of cloth that the friars wear hanging from the neck, bearing a pouch that contains a holy image. In four of the other panels there are angels carrying scapulars and flowers among the clouds and, in those at the corners, four allegorical figures of the Virtues.

In the short passage that connects the two side rooms on this floor there is a strong picture of 'Judith and Holofernes' by Piazzetta.

The Campo Santa Margherita, into which you come if you turn left when you leave the School, has in its centre an 18th century building, the Scuola dei Varotari (tanners) with a good early-Renaissance relief of the 'Virgin and Worshippers' on its north wall. On the west side of the Campo are some attractive buildings, especially two small early houses

31A   Santa Maria del Carmelo. The 'Deposition' by Francesco di Giorgio

31B Santa Maria del Carmelo, 'St Nicholas in Glory' by Lotto

next to one another (Nos. 2931 to 2935), restored but with 13th and 14th century features. That on the left (Nos. 2931 and 2932) has an ambitious doorway for so small a house, and both have good windows, placed not symmetrically but elegantly, and old-fashioned projecting roofs.

(Also in Index of Artists: Balestra, Bambini, Zanchi.)

Santa Maria della Fava R 6

An 18th century building. The angels holding the holy-water stoups are pretty but *innominati*. The saints between the pillars are by Bernardi, who was Canova's teacher, and so are the bas-reliefs above them. The first picture on the right is an excellent early one (1732) by Tiepolo of the 'Virgin as a Child with St Anne and St Joachim'. The second on the left is an even better one (1726) by Piazzetta of 'St Philip Neri praying to the Virgin and Child'. Both were well cleaned for the special exhibition 'Ricci to Tiepolo' in Venice in 1969. Tiepolo's is a gentle scene based on the contrasting age of St Anne and youth of the Virgin. He was still under some influence from Piazzetta, but his palette is already lighter. Piazzetta has used all his skill in colour and design, and even if the Virgin is a portrait of a vain Venetian, the brilliant sway of the composition, starting from the blue cloak held away by an angel against the pale russet sky, following with the brightness of the Virgin's robe and coming back to the subdued tones of the saint, is complemented by the play of colour, thrilling though mostly brown and red.

From the bridge outside the church you can see on the left (with your back to the church) the grand façade of the Palazzo Giustiniani Faccanon, 15th century Gothic, not spoilt by the row of 18th century figures on top.

Santa Maria Formosa W Cas: 6

This handsome church with an unconventional exterior is both completely Renaissance and completely Venetian, and was rebuilt in 1492 on the plans of Mauro Coducci. On the west side you can see a vile mask below the 17th century baroque campanile, a pretty little 'Madonna and Child' of about 1450 on the low building between the campanile and the main church, and over the main door a statue of Vincenzo Cappello, who defeated the Turks in 1541, and whose family paid for the facade.

Inside, the architecture is open and attractive. Over the font on the right, too high to be seen comfortably, is a small round picture of the 'Circumcision', ascribed sometimes to Catena, but certainly by a weaker painter who derived from Giovanni Bellini. In the first chapel on the right is a triptych by Bartolomeo Vivarini in good preservation, much hampered by the entirely unsuitable marble surround. In the centre of it is the 'Madonna and the Faithful' and on either side the 'Birth of the Virgin' and the 'Meeting of Joachim and Anna'. In the next chapel is a picture of 'The Pietà and St Francis', which is a much more successful example of Palma Giovane's painting than many dozens of other works by him in Venice. In the right transept on the left is the 'Gunners' Chapel' with a really beautiful picture of 'St Barbara' painted by Palma Vecchio when, as a young man, he was almost keeping pace with Giorgione and Titian (Plate 34). There are other pictures by him round it, the 'Dead Christ' above, 'St Sebastian' and 'St John the Baptist' on the right, 'St Antony' and 'St Dominic' on the left. The whole group is fortunately in excellent preservation.

In the second chapel on the left of the chancel is a ciborium with a fairly good late 16th century statue of 'The Redeemer' with angels at either side, and a dreadfully weak picture of 'The Circumcision' by a poor imitator of Cima da Conegliano.

(Also in Index of Artists: Campagna, Torretti.)

The Campo in which the church stands has some old buildings in it including on the east side, No. 5246, the Palazzo Vitturi, with a rather untidy 13th century façade, and higher up, No. 6126, the Palazzo Doria, 15th century, with a larger unnamed neighbour, No. 6124. On the south side is the early 16th century Palazzo Malipiero-Trevisan, ruined by a modern excrescence on top.

Down the Ruga Giuffa, which leads out of the south-east corner of the Campo, you can see at the end of the first alley on the left (Ramo Grimani) the doorway of the Palazzo Grimina, mid 16th century, perhaps by Sanmicheli, burdened with three bad classical heads. At the end of the fourth alley (Ramo dell'Arco), you get a glimpse of the 13th century Palazzo Bon. Turning left at the Salizzada Zorzi you pass Coducci's Palazzo Zorzi (not to be confused with the older Palazzo Zorzi by the Ponte dei Greci), and from the bridge (of S. Severo) you can see its main façade up the canal and beyond it the fine façade of the P. Bon and the dull facade of the P. Grimani.

32   Scuola di Santa Maria del Carmine. 'St Simon Stock receiving
the Scapular' by Tiepolo

Santa Maria del Giglio (or Zobenigo)   SM 7

This church had a 14th century campanile, but it fell in 1774 and the small picture-gallery next to the church is made out of its base. The facade of the church was designed by Sardi and built around 1680 to the order and the glory of the naval family called Barbaro. It is a supreme example of Venetian baroque. Five Barbaros appear on the facade below naval and military trophies, and on the base are reliefs of Rome and Padua and of naval cities, Zara, Spalato, Candia and Corfu. Ruskin called it 'the most impious building, illustrative of the degradation of the Renaissance'.

Inside, on the right, against the entrance wall and beyond a small broken Lombard relief of St Jerome, is a 16th century figure of 'The Redeemer'. Along the right wall, a door leads into a room now used as the oratory, in which are a Venetian-Byzantine picture of the 'Virgin and Child' and a very fine late 18th century ivory crucifix with St Mary Magdalene at the side below. In the next chapel but one the double basin, now embellished with a baroque lid and swags, is said to be ancient Greek. In the following chapel is 'St Mary Magdalene' by Zanchi. In the sacristy is the altar from which the statue of the Redeemer (see above) was removed, leaving two angels, and below it a relief of the head of St John the Baptist as a child, sometimes wrongly ascribed to Desiderio da Settignano, but certainly Tuscan. Also there is a picture of 'Abraham partitioning the World' by Zanchi, and a 'Holy Family' alleged to be by Rubens.

A door in the sacristy leads to the chancel and thus affords an opportunity of seeing a pair of organ screens, with two Evangelists on each, by Tintoretto, somewhat restored but vigorous and successful. The sacristan will turn on lights to show them.

Back to the nave, on the left wall as you return towards the main door first on the right is another picture by Tintoretto, of the 'Saviour with St Justina and St Augustine', never very striking and much damaged by restorers. Over the last altar, there is a mediocre picture of the 'Martyrdom of St Antony' by Zanchi.

(Also in Index of Artists: Marieschi, Palma Giovane, Vittoria.)

Santa Maria Mater Domini   SC 8

This little church has now been closed and its pictures have been removed. I am told that the closure is for repairs, and so it may be reopened in a few years' time. If you make for it by vaporetto it is closest to San Stae, but you can also reach it from the Rialto; you can then see S. Giacomo di Rialto, S. Giovanni Elemosinario and S. Cassiano on the way.

It was consecrated in 1540 and is a simple early Renaissance building tending towards Florentine style. There is a small 14th century Byzantine half-length figure of the Virgin over the door.

Inside on the right wall of the nave is one of Vincenzo Catena's last successes, 'St Christina', not a supreme work but quite charming (Plate 35). It must be the mildest martyrdom in all pictorial hagiography. The Saint is kneeling on the shore before being thrown into the sea with a millstone attached to a rope round her neck. Five enchanting angels are attending her and two of them have got control of the rope and the millstone. Above her she sees her Lord waiting for her, and before Him a sixth angel bearing the white robe of martyrdom that is ready for her as soon as the formal ordeal is over. The picture has been well restored recently.

The 'Last Supper' over the side door is by Bonifzaio. In the left transept is Tintoretto's 'Finding of the True Cross', robustly painted but a clumsy, unsuccessful conception. Under it is a 13th century marble bas-relief of the 'Virgin at Prayer' very Byzantine. On the right of the nave near the door, and in the chapel to the left of the chancel, there are fairly good early 16th century altar-pieces by Lorenzo Bregno, all the small statues on them being by him except 'St Andrew' on the one by the door. The 'Transfiguration' on the left wall of the nave is by Bissolo.

Santa Maria dei Miracoli (Plate 36)   E Can: 6

This is an exceptional church in that it was designed and decorated all in one operation between 1480 and 1490 by the Lombardi and has no discordant later additions or alterations. It is one of the most beautiful small churches in the world. Nothing really needs special mention because of the sense of completeness inside and outside, and no one can fail to see the handsome wooden screen of the 'barco' (that is, the monks' choir over the door), the exquisite carved marble altar rails in the raised chancel, the four little half-figures of the Virgin, the Archangel Gabriel, St Francis and St Clare on its balustrade, and the fine gilt wooden ceiling, the pictures on which are apt but not of any great

33   Santa Maria della Fava. 'St Philip Neri praying to the Virgin and Child' by Piazzetta

artistic value. On the High Altar is the miraculous picture of the Virgin that gives the church its name, and on either side are two bronze statues by Vittoria, St Peter and St Antony Abbot, which are the only later additions, but entirely appropriate, since Vittoria here used the style of the Lombardi. In the sacristy are St Francis and St Clare again, this time by Campagna.

Leaving the church, just down the little campo on the left is the Fondamenta Sanudo and, if you look to your left where it crosses a canal, you can see, though only partially, the Palazzo Soranzo, one of the finest of Venetian palaces. Ruskin calls it 14th century though in fact it was rebuilt in the second half of the 15th with many of the features of the earlier building incorporated in it, including the oldest wooden door in the city, with its original knocker in the form of a fish.

Santa Maria della Salute   ED 7

This, the most conspicuous church in Venice after St Mark's, was built between 1681 and 1687, a few years before and after the death of Longhena, who designed it. It had taken fifty years to prepare the ground for the building, the decision to build a church having been taken by the city before the great plague of 1630 had finished, as a votive offering therefore to hasten its end rather than as a thanksgiving for its being over. *Salute* means either 'health' or 'salvation'. Longhena's design won the competition which had been arranged for the building and which laid down, among other conditions, that it should be showy but not too expensive. The result is this dashing example of Venetian Baroque architecture.

Inside, the architecture is more conventional, and it deserves contemplation. There are three altar-pieces on the right, all by Luca Giordano, and over the altar on the left nearest the chancel, a 'Descent of the Holy Ghost' by Titian, which is a late work spoiled by restoration. The best pictures are in the sacristy. On the wall opposite the window is Tintoretto's 'Marriage in Cana', enormously admired by Ruskin and an ambitious and successful adventure in light and perspective Over the altar, 'St Mark surrounded by SS. Cosmas and Damian, Roch and Sebastian', painted by Titian when a young man, in 1511 or 1512. Ruskin said that it has been ruined by restoration, but since his day it had been cleaned and properly restored and is in no bad way. On the

34   Santa Maria Formosa. 'St Barbara' by Palma Vecchio

roof are three very dramatic pictures, 'David and Goliath', 'The Sacrifice of Isaac', and 'Cain and Abel', also painted by Titian but later, between 1540 and 1550. Ruskin thought them disgusting, but one cannot think why, except that Goliath's neck is severed. The heads round the altar are also by Titian, and one is a self-portrait, the others being various saints. All these pictures were originally in a church called Santo Spirito, and were brought here when it was pulled down. On the front of the altar itself is a marvellous piece of tapestry of the 15th century. Back in the church, on the left as you come out of the sacristy, there is a handsome bronze candlestick by Andrea Bresciano, *c.* 1570. The group on the High Altar is reckoned to be good Baroque sculpture.

(Also in Index of Artists: Palma Giovane, Tullio Lombardo.)

Santa Maria Zobenigo
See Santa Maria del Giglio.

San Martino   W Cas: 17
Designed by Sansovino. Inside, next to the pulpit is an altar table, with angels for legs, by Tullio Lombardo. 'St Martin in Glory' on the ceiling is by Guarana, and there are tabernacle panels by Palma Giovane in the sacristy (ruined).

San Marziale   W Can: 10
A late 17th century building of no architectural importance. The second picture on the right wall of the nave of the saint between St Peter and St Paul is by Tintoretto, but heavily repainted, and the 'Death of St Joseph' on the left wall (chancel end) is by Antonio Balestra. Just outside either side of the chancel there are the 'Madonna' and the 'Angel of the Annunciation' by Tintoretto's son Domenico. In the sacristy is a badly restored picture of 'The Archangel Raphael with St Tobias' by Titian.

The pictures on the ceiling, one in the chancel and three in the main part, are by Sebastiano Ricci. They were painted before 1705, and are of great historical importance because they are the first ceiling pictures in the 18th century style which was to be taken up and developed so well by Tiepolo. Nothing so light had been painted before, not at least for a hundred years. They hark back across the dark 17th century to Veronese, but the palette is even lighter than his, and it set the key for the new generation. The subject in the chancel is

35   Santa Maria Mater Domini. 'St Christina' by Catena

36 Santa Maria dei Miracoli

'God the Father' and the other three represent 'St Martial in Glory', a 'Miraculous Appearance of an Image of the Virgin', and the 'Virgin's Image carved on a Tree'.

(Also in Index of Artists: Zanchi.)

San Michele
See Murano

The Misericordia   W Can: 11
There are three buildings, a double one comprising the church and abbey, the old school and the new school. The church and abbey have nothing left in them. On the facade of these, which are mid 17th century, are some unimportant statues, and on the right a 14th century Byzantine bas-relief of the Madonna. The old school, next to the church and abbey and at right angles to them, has a 15th century Gothic façade, gaunt but handsome. On it are two small angels by Bartolomeo Bon, the remains of a relief of the 'Adoration of the Virgin' the main part of which is now in the Victoria and Albert Museum in London. There is said to be an elegant small cloister between the buildings. The huge new school across the bridge from the old one was designed by Sansovino and has never been finished.

San Moisè   SM 12
The building is mid 17th century and the flamboyant baroque façade was constructed in 1668. Of the pictures inside, that on the ceiling of 'Jehovah and Moses' by Nicolò Bambini and two on the entrance wall by Brusaferro (right) and Sante Piatti (left) of the 'Crucifixion' and 'Stoning of St Stephen' are helpful to those who wish to weigh the merits of 17th and 18th century Venetians, because they have recently been very well cleaned. The 'Virgin and St Antony of Padua' on the ceiling of the chapel on the right of the chancel is by Guarana.

In the chapel on the left of the chancel high up on the left wall is a late poor picture by Tintoretto, of 'Christ washing His Disciples' Feet', added to by restorers and very hard to see. In the sacristy, on the front of the altar, is a splendid bas-relief by Nicolò and Sebastiano Roccatagliata, representing the 'Descent from the Cross' and the 'Dead Christ borne by Angels'.

Murano and San Michele
Murano is the largest of the islands north of Venice, famous for its glass. There is a glass museum with very fine antique exhibits and there are many factories with sale-rooms.

On the way to Murano lies the cemetery island of S. Michele, whose beautiful Renaissance church was designed by Mauro Coducci and built under his constant supervision in the 1470s. The pretty statue of the 'Virgin and Child' over the door is somewhat earlier. The hexagonal chapel that leads off from the church is later, about 1530, and was designed by Guglielmo dei Grigi and finished by Sansovino. The cloisters are 15th century and well preserved.

The parish church of Murano is San Pietro Martire, in the centre of the island. It was built in the first years of the 16th century, was closed and emptied early in the 19th. Its present contents have thus been acquired since it was reopened in 1813. Because there was a Gothic church on the site before this one, the shape is Gothic, there are some 15th century frescoes between the arches in the nave, and the roof is mainly of this earlier date. On the right wall is an 'Assumption of the Virgin, with eight Saints' (Peter, John, Mark, Francis, Louis, Antony Abbot, Augustine and John the Baptist) against a wide landscape, by Giovanni Bellini and his assistants. It is a late picture, and, however much of it is not by the hand of the master himself, his skills are in it, such as the accuracy in depicting various surfaces in various lights and the rôle of the barren tree, just behind the foreground, cutting the middle-distance horseman, the battlements further back, and finally the clouds and the sky, to mark the recession of the scene. It is a pity that because of its position and its uneven surface the picture is hard to see. Next to it is a truly beautiful picture by Bellini's own hand, of the 'Presentation of Doge Barbarigo to the Madonna by St Mark, with St Augustine', which is dated 1488. This is the year of the Frari Triptych, and the Madonna is the same country girl with large heavy-lidded eyes. She is quite detached from the proceedings, but the Infant Christ is smiling down at the Doge. Besides the peacock on the right there are a peahen and a stork. The group is grandly set, the Virgin and Child against the green back of the throne, the musicians, saints and the Doge against red curtains with the luminous background on either side.

Beyond this is a 'Baptism of Christ' perhaps by Tintoretto with much studio assistance. In the chapel on the left of the

37A San Moise. The 'Descent from the Cross' by Roccatagliata

chancel there is a tasteful Renaissance marble altar-piece. As you come back along the left side of the nave there is first, over the sacristy door, a picture of 'St Jerome in the Desert' by Paolo Veronese, said to be damaged, but in fact in no bad way, and then another picture by him of 'St Agatha in Prison, visited by St Peter and an Angel'.

The church of Santa Maria degli Angeli, up in the north-west part of the island, was rebuilt in the 16th century. It has a beautiful Renaissance bas-relief over the entrance to its forecourt, shamefully stained for want of an inexpensive protection against rain-water. Inside there is a 16th century painted ceiling, and, in the chancel, a boisterous 'Annunciation' by Pordenone and a monument to Jacopo Soranzo by Vittoria. But the church, which is miserably unkempt in every way, is only open on some Sunday mornings.

SS. Maria e Donato, near the glass museum, is a 12th century Venetian-Byzantine building, whose architectural beauty and interest have not been entirely spoilt by 19th century restoration. Inside there is a remarkable mosaic floor (Plate 37B), dated 1140, and a fine 12th century mosaic wall-piece of the 'Virgin in Prayer', covering the apse in the chancel, with 14th century frescoes below. On the left wall of the nave, first, as you come back from the chancel end, is a Venetian-Byzantine painting of the 'Madonna' above, and below a 14th century polyptych. Then, over the door to the baptistery is a good semi-circular picture by Lazzaro Bastiani of the 'Virgin and Saints and the Donor', and finally a painted wooden bas-relief of St Donatus, dated 1310, with small portraits of the donor and his wife at either end of its base.

The glass museum is well labelled. It has a few unimportant pictures, the best a 'Crucifixion' by Leonardo Corona,

37B   Murano, SS. Maria e Donato. Mosaic floor (detail)

and those painted on glass at least as attractive as the rest.

(Also in Index of Artists: Palma Giovane, B. Vivarini, Zanchi.)

San Nicolò dei Mendicoli WD 1

Founded as early as the 7th century, this little church is now a mélange of styles from then on, but the mixture is so great that in the end the interior is quite engaging. The oldest part is the chancel, which is 12th century. Then come the columns and wooden roof, visible in the aisles at each side of the nave, and in the transepts, 13th and 14th century. And next the arches in the transepts, which are 15th century. The whole interior is however swamped by the late 16th century carved and gilt woodwork over the pillars and round the organ.

The pictures of the Life of Christ along the walk are by Veronese's nephew, Alvise del Friso, except the 'Resurrection', which is by Palma Giovane. The side pictures on the ceiling of acts of St Nicholas are by Leonardo Corona. Behind the altar table in the chancel is a gilt 15th century carving of St Nicholas.

Outside there is an old portico where poor virtuous women used to be very inadequately housed, or at least sheltered. The square 12th century Veneto-Byzantine campanile has lost its cupola.

San Nicolò da Tolentino SC 2

A robust building by Scamozzi in the style of Palladio, finished just after 1600 except for the classical colonnaded facade which is 18th century. Of the many pictures it contains, the most interesting are the 'Charity of St

Laurence', by Bernardo Strozzi, over the door near the chancel on the left, and 'St Jerome' by Giovanni Lyss (or Johann Lis), on the narrow lateral wall on the left just outside the chancel. The High Altar is by Longhena, but not the clumsy angels on either side of it.

(Also in Index of Artists: Palma Giovane, Peranda, Pitati.)

Cà d'Oro
See under 'Cà'

The Ospedaletto (properly Santa Maria dei Derelitti or dell' Ospedaletto)   W Cas: 4
By Longhena, who designed all the altars. Full of late 17th century and early 18th century pictures, one, the fourth on the right of those over the arches, 'Abraham and Isaac', by Tiepolo.

This church is commonly known as the Ospedaletto. The actual hostel from which it gets its name adjoins it, and contains an oval staircase by Sardi and a pretty music-room.

(Also in Index of Artists: Guarana, Palma Giovane.)

San Pantaleone*   SP 5

This church contains a huge ceiling painting by G. A. Fumiani, who took twenty-four years (1680-1704) over it. It roused Ruskin to a fury of indignation at its vulgarity. Outside the first chapel on the right, in the spaces above the arch, are 'St Philip' and 'St Bartholomew' by Guarana. At the back of the second chapel on the right is a picture of 'St Pantaleon curing a Sick Child', by Paolo Veronese. On the left wall of the next chapel is another picture partly by him and partly by his assistants, of 'St Bernardino founding a Hospital'. And the altar-piece in this chapel, 'St Bernardino receiving the Symbol of Christ', is ascribed to him by Berenson. The two little paintings over the arch of the chapel, 'St Thaddeus' and 'St Matthew', are by Alessandro Longhi, and beyond, by Guarana, is 'Christ and St Mary Magdalene'. In the chancel the High Altar is by Sardi. The paintings on the ceiling and the back wall are by Fumiani. Outside, 'Charity' (above) is by Alessandro Longhi and the 'Supper at Emmaus' (below) is by Guarana.

*The name of 'San Pantaleone' is a corruption of St Panteleemon (Greek for 'all merciful'), who was a Christian doctor martyred by Diocletian and a patron saint of doctors, ranking here in Venice next to St Luke.

In the chapel on the left of the chancel the picture of the 'Coronation of the Virgin' is by Antonio Vivarini and Giovanni d'Alemagna. The altar here is made up, fairly successfully, of early 15th century Gothic carvings. Over the arch of the nearest chapel on the left of the nave, 'St Peter' and 'St Andrew' are by Pietro Longhi. The altar-piece of the last chapel is the 'Immaculate Conception' by Bambini, and beyond it high up in the corner are 'Prudence' and 'Justice' by Alessandro Longhi. Below the former, and so just above the recess that holds the font, is 'Christ casting out a Devil' by Angelo Trevisani.

(Also in Index of Artists: Balestra, Fumiani, Palma Giovane.)

Seminario Patriarcale
See Pinacoteca Manfrediana.

La Pietà (or Santa Maria della Pietà)   W Cas: 11
This is an 18th century church, but its facade was built in 1906 from the original design. Inside it is of a pleasant oval shape. On the ceiling are two fine paintings by Tiepolo. The large and splendid one, in the centre of the main ceiling, is of 'The Triumph of Faith', and that over the High Altar is of 'The Cardinal Virtues'.

The picture of the 'Visitation' on the High Altar was started by Piazzetta but finished by a pupil of his called Giuseppe Angeli, whose colouring was not as subtle as Piazzetta's. In the raised choir over the door, to enter which you need the help of the sacristan, is a picture by Moretto of Brescia of the 'Feast in the House of Simon', which is well worth the effort to see. If you cannot get the sacristan to take you up to it, it looks very well with its light on from the chancel steps.

Incidentally, the pictures over the first two altars on the left are not by Piazzetta, but they are in his manner and by his pupils, the first by Giuseppe Angeli and the second by Antonio Marinetti.

San Pietro di Castello   E Cas: 4
This was the cathedral church of Venice until 1807. The façade is of Palladian type and was constructed in 1596. The campanile is by Coducci except for the cupola, which is a later replacement. Inside, third on the right wall of the nave is 'St Peter and Four Saints' by Basaiti, and on the left are a 'Madonna' by Luca Giordano (in the chapel) and a late picture

38A
La Pietà. The 'Feast in the House
of Simon' (detail) by Moretto

by Veronese of 'St John, St Peter and St Paul'. The High
Altar is by Longhena. In the chapel to the left of the chancel
there is a primitive beaten copper crucifix, Venetian-Byzantine of the beginning of the 14th century.

San Polo   SP 7

This is a 15th century Gothic church, of straightforward
design. On the outside of the door on the south side by
which you enter are three simple pieces of sculpture, an angel
on either side and a half-figure of St Paul on the apex of the
arch, all contemporary with the building. On the wall of the
14th century campanile near this door are two lions,
probably 15th century, one with a serpent, and the other
with a human head between its forepaws.

The interior was spoiled by renovation in 1804, and later
attempts to restore and reveal the original have not been able
to efface the results of the damage so done. But the small
rose window, high up on the main entrance wall, was not
damaged or altered.

On this main entrance wall (though in fact you enter by
the side door described above), on the left of the door as you
face it inside, is one of Tintoretto's 'Last Suppers', an
exercise in striking composition, with every figure dramatically posed and every face dramatically strained. The picture
near it on the right wall of the nave, of 'The Assumption', is a
very weak affair by one of Tintoretto's assistants. In the
vestibule are the 'Stations of the Cross', painted by Domenico Tiepolo, and the picture above those on the right, of a
'Glory of Angels', is by him also.

On either side of the High Altar are bronze statues of 'St
Paul' and 'St Antony Abbot' by Vittoria. In the chapel on
the left of the chancel the picture on the main altar of 'The
Betrothal of the Virgin and Angels' is by Veronese, late and
in bad comdition. The picture of St John Nepomuk (S.
Giovanni Nepomuceno*), next but one to the side door on
the left of the nave, is by G. B. Tiepolo.

In the north-west corner of the Campo is Sanmicheli's
classical Palazzo Corner-Mocenigo, with its main facade, on
the Rio di S. Polo, visible from the bridge down the street

*The saint was martyred by being thrown over a bridge in Prague, where he was an
Augustinian canon, for refusing to betray secrets of the confessional. In Austria
and Bohemia he thus became the patron saint of silence and also of bridges and
rivers. A crown with five stars above it was said to have appeared where he died,
and he is often represented, though not here, with a crown in his hand, five stars
above his head and sometimes with his finger to his lips or a padlock on his
mouth.

from the church door. On the east side at the south end is a late 15th century corner window and higher up are one or two early palazzi.

Out of the north-east corner leads the Calle Bernardo, and at its bridge is the main door of the 15th century Gothic Palazzo Bernardo, a truly splendid palace which Ruskin called the noblest in Venice after the Ducal Palace.

(Also in Index of Artists: Palma Giovane.)

Galleria Querini-Stampalia   W Cas: 7

Do not miss the naive but delightful pictures of 18th century Venetian life by Gabriele Bella in the room to the left of the entrance hall. In the other early rooms there is only one interesting picture, a Venetian-Gothic primitive by Donato and Catarino, dated 1372, in *Room II,* though the two large portraits by Sebastiano Bombelli in *Room III* have a certain spirit, and in *Room VII* there is a maquette by Canova for a portrait of Napoleon's mother. In *Room VIII* there is an early fresh picture of the 'Presentation' by Giovanni Bellini, almost identical with one by Mantegna in Berlin. Also here are a 'Madonna and Child' in his style but probably not by him, two good unfinished portraits of Francesco Querini and his bride, Paola Priuli, by Palma Vecchio (Plate 38B), and an 'Adoration' by Verrocchio's Florentine pupil, Lorenzo di Credi, who painted it when he was in Venice helping Verrocchio with the Colleoni statue.

In *Room IX* is a fine picture of 'Judith' by Catena (Plate 39). Not Judith really, but a handsome young woman, with a sword at her side and a severed head in front of her, dressed in a clean white blouse with a crimson velvet cloak against a grey background with a green balustrade in front. Also in this room is a 'Holy Family with St John, St Catherine, St Dominic and St Nicholas' by Paris Bordone.

Rooms XI, XII and *XIII* are given over to Pietro Longhi. In *Room XI* the 'Sagredo Family' is as good as his doll-like portrait groups ever are, the 'Michiel Family' much inferior, the monks and friars and fashionable scenes (Mondo Novo, the dance called La Furlana, the Masked Party) all with Longhi's limitations but with his chief merit, that of making a good pattern of pretty colours, and indeed it goes rather further than just that. Alas, he attempted the 'Temptation of St Antony', and it is a shame to hang it here in a public gallery. The Seven Sacraments in *Room XII* (Baptism, Confirmation, Confession, Communion, Marriage, Holy Orders, Extreme Unction) are better than any pictures in *Room XI,* but the 'Geography Lesson' and another version of the 'Masked Party' are feeble. There are also two lions. In *Room XIII* the bird-shooting scenes are darker and stronger than all the rest (so much so that one authority doubts that they are Longhi's) but the peasant scenes are poor stuff poorly preserved.

In *Room XIV,* skied, is a small dark picture of 'St Francis' by Piazzetta's epigone, Federico Bencovich.

In the rest of the rooms are some portraits, in *Room XVIII* one of a 'Procurator', by G. B. Tiepolo, and another of Daniele Dolfin, by Alessandro Longhi, both good 18th century works. In *Room XIX* are two vigorous 17th century pictures, one of the 'Virgin and Child' by Bernardo Strozzi, the other of 'The Death of Croton' by Francesco Maffei.

(Also in Index of Artists: *Room IV* Palma Giovane, *Room V* Schiavone, *Room VI* Zanchi, *Room IX* Palma Vecchio.)

The Redentore   G 2

This is one of Palladio's masterpieces, though seen from any angle except full front the main structure looks clumsy compared with the façade, which Mr. Raymond Mortimer has described as 'frozen music'. Inside, the architecture, which is splendidly successful, is virtually all that is worth mentioning. In the sacristy is a good 'Virgin and Child' by Alvise Vivarini in his most Bellinesque mood, kept behind wooden doors. Otherwise there is no picture of any merit, the so-called Veronese, also in the sacristy, and the so-called Tintorettos on the right and left walls of the nave being all poor school pictures. The crucifix on the High Altar, and the statues on either side of it, of 'St Francis' and 'St Mark', are by Campagna.

(Also in Index of Artists: Bastiani, Palma Giovane.)

Cà Rezzonico

See under 'Cà'

Church of San Rocco   SP 2

The original building was late 15th century, but it was reconstructed between 1765 and 1771. It contains several pictures by Tintoretto. On the entrance wall are 'The Annunciation' and 'St Roch before the Pope', both by him and once a pair of organ doors. Ruskin admired the figure of

39   Galleria Querini-Stampalia. 'Judith' by Catena

the Pope in the latter, but nothing else in it, and described the former, rather unfairly seeing how graceful the angel is, as 'a most disagreeable and dead picture'. On the right wall of the nave first of all is a characteristic picture by Sebastiano Ricci of 'St Francis restoring a child to life'. Next is 'The Pool of Bethesda' by Tintoretto, once a pair of cupboard doors, seriously damaged and added to. Above, also credited to Tintoretto by Berenson, but perhaps partly by his assistants, is a battle scene with St Roch on the left being led off to prison.

The High Altar's decoration dates from about 1500, and the three small pictures on the coffin which contains St Roch's corpse may be by Andrea Schiavone (though they are not ascribed to him by Berenson). Two putti right and left of the altar are remains of frescoes by Pordenone. There are four pictures by Tintoretto on the walls of the chancel, those below representing 'St Roch healing in a Hospital' (on the right) and 'St Roch in Prison comforted by an Angel' (on the left), both huge, competent and unattractive. 'St Roch healing Animals', above on the left, is so weak that it must be largely a school work. 'St Roch in the Desert', above on the right, has a contrived and uninteresting landscape background.

In the corridor from the left transept to the sacristy is a fresco of 'St Sebastian' by Pordenone. On the left wall of the nave are 'St Martin and St Christopher with Suppliants', by Pordenone, and 'St Helena with the True Cross' by Ricci.

(Also in Index of Artists: Fumiani.)

Scuola di San Rocco   SP 3

The change in architecture that took place in Venice in the first half of the 16th century is written on the façade of the school, which was designed and built by Bartolomeo Bon (of Bergamo) to start with and then, after a pause between 1524 and 1527, by Scarpagnino. The lower order of the façade is mostly Bon's, but the columns and the door, besides all of the upper order, belong to Scarpagnino, who completed the building in 1549. It houses the great series of pictures painted for it by Tintoretto. These were immensely admired for a century or two, but when Ruskin managed to get into the school to see them in 1845 they were in a sad state of neglect, with rain allowed to fall on some through holes in the roof. They have been better treated since then and are mostly in good condition again, except for some restoration here and there and some excessive fading of those that were hung where full sunlight fell on them.*

There are between fifty and sixty pictures in three rooms. The best, and one of the greatest in the world, 'The Crucifixion', is in the smaller room on the upper floor called the Sala dell'Albergo. Next best are those on the ground floor, which are more carefully painted than those in the main upper room except for 'The Temptation' and 'The Last Supper' there.

The series on the ground floor, which was painted last, between 1583 and 1587, starts with the picture that faces you as you enter, the 'Annunciation'. It is an astonishing conception, the Virgin being seated in a ruined house with carpenters' tools and materials lying about and the angel appearing to her through a window frame. Curiously enough, the Virgin's face is handsome enough when seen close up, but from a normal distance, as Ruskin pointed out, seems unattractive and pained. Otherwise, this is a fine picture, full of life, 'the execution' being, in Ruskin's words, 'carried to the utmost limits of boldness consistent with completion'.

Next is the 'Adoration of the Magi', which Ruskin called 'the most finished picture in the Scuola, except the Crucifixion, and perhaps the most delightful of the whole'. He also pointed out that the composition of it is based on the light and is star-shaped, with the Infant Christ as the centre, and that a judicious break is made in its symmetry by the luminous background and the line of ghostly horsemen there. But this line of light, the brick column on the right, the man with outstretched arms in the right foreground and two other lay figures are only there to carry out the composition. The two white Magi are so out of key that they must be portraits.

Third is the 'Flight into Egypt', in which Tintoretto made amends for the 'Annunciation' by the beauty of the Virgin's head. The donkey is a masterpiece in itself, and the landscape good in mass and in detail, though the clump in the centre, even after cleaning, looks confused. The rough fence, of sticks and string, on the right in the foreground, is an example of Tintoretto's brilliant depiction of things seen by him in their true nature, with the utmost economy in the painting of them. This was what really appealed to Ruskin.

*The Edgar J. Kaufmann Charitable Foundation, of Pittsburgh, by a gift to the International Fund for Monuments, started a programme of cleaning and restoration in 1969. The restoration was completed in 1975.

Fourth is the 'Massacre of the Innocents', and the noticeable thing about Tintoretto's treatment of this horrible subject (all too popular with artists) is that there is no stabbing, no cutting and no blood.

At the end of this and the opposite wall, next to the windows, are two narrow pictures, 'The Magdalen' and 'St Mary of Egypt', both painted in tones of brown and gold. The composition of each, based on its landscape and centred on a huge tree and a relatively small figure, is tranquil like the colour. St Mary of Egypt sits at the side of her canvas, with a beautifully painted stream before her. The tree in the 'Magdalen' is marred by the most casual handling of its branches.

We are now round to the entrance wall, and the next picture is of the 'Circumcision', carefully painted, dignified, and said to be influenced by the style of Veronese.

The last picture, the 'Assumption of the Virgin', is more than half repainted. The circle of cherubs is original, and the design, with the horizontal angel strongly supporting it, can be visualised, but otherwise the picture is not worth lingering over.

The statue of St Roch on the altar in this room is by Campagna and so is late 16th century. The staircase leading to the upper floor is by Scarpagnino, perhaps with some help or advice from Sansovino.

The main upper room has its walls and ceiling covered with pictures by Tintoretto, but there are other things in it worth looking at. On the altar, on either side of Tintoretto's damaged altar-piece of 'St Roch in Glory', are statues by Campagna of 'St John the Baptist' and 'St Sebastian'. At the corners of the choir-screen are unfinished statues by him of two prophets. On easels at the altar end are an 'Annunciation' by Titian and a 'Visitation' by Tintoretto, both very beautiful, and also two most attractive pictures by Tiepolo, painted when he was young and had not developed his more characteristic style, one of 'Abraham with the Angels, and the other of 'Hagar succoured by Angels'. Along the wall that faces you as you enter are some excellent 17th century wooden carvings by Francesco Pianta, who is otherwise virtually unknown, including a portrait of himself unmasking his face, a spy with his face half hidden under a large spy's hat, and a caricature of Tintoretto. Lastly, on an easel just outside the door which leads into the smaller Sala dell' Albergo is a self-portrait by Tintoretto of marvellous quality, dated 1573.

The pictures on the walls and ceiling are mostly more hastily painted than those in the lower room or in the Sala dell' Albergo. They were done under contract between 1576 and 1581, most of them in the last three years. They are thus earlier than those in the lower room, and later than the 'Crucifixion' and the rest in the Sala, the dates of which lie within 1564, 1565 and 1566. The order of those on the walls is haphazard. If you turn right as you enter, the two on the entrance wall are 'The Raising of Lazarus' and 'The Miracle of the Loaves and Fishes'. On the opposite wall, that at the end on the right is one of the many 'Last Suppers' that Tintoretto painted, a remarkable composition in three dimensions with Christ and the Apostles set dramatically in shadow between light foreground and background. Then, from right to left are 'The Agony in the Garden' (which Ruskin suggested had been painted in two hours with a broom for a brush), 'The Resurrection', 'The Baptism of Christ' and 'The Adoration of the Shepherds'. On the window wall are 'St Roch' and 'St Sebastian', of which Ruskin thought the former rather coarse, the latter remarkably fine. Next, coming round to the entrance wall again, is 'The Temptation', no doubt the best of this series, with Satan represented as young, handsome and well fed, but given away by his cloven hooves. Between the two doorways are 'The Pool of Bethesda' and 'The Ascension'.

The ceiling is painted with Old Testament scenes, boldly designed and rapidly painted. Straight down the centre from the altar end to the window end are alternately four narrow and three larger pictures of 'The Passover', 'The Fall of Manna', 'The Sacrifice of Isaac', 'Moses and Aaron and the Brazen Serpent', 'Jonah', 'Moses striking the Rock' and 'Adam and Eve'. The three on the side nearest the doorways, in similar order, are of 'Elijah distributing Bread', 'Jacob's Ladder' and 'The Passage of the Red Sea', and those on the other side are of 'Elijah fed by Angels', 'The Vision of Ezekiel' and 'God appearing to Moses'.

In the Sala dell'Albergo 'The Crucifixion' overpowers all the rest. But one of the easel pictures of 'Christ carrying the Cross' is notable because it was once believed to be miraculous and also because it has always puzzled the experts, who still have not agreed whether it is by Titian or by Giorgione, Berenson giving it to the latter. The other, of the 'Dead Christ', is now usually thought to be an early work by Titian in Giorgionesque style. In a frame in front of 'The Crucifixion' is a piece of canvas found doubled over when

Tintoretto's frieze in this room was being cleaned and restored, and thus showing how bright his colours originally were.

When the fraternity first decided to have the school decorated with pictures, they arranged a competition. On the judging day, Veronese and others brought their drawings, but Tintoretto proceeded to unveil the central picture in the ceiling of 'St Roch in Glory', which he had painted as his entry for the competition and had secretly had installed where it now is. It is thus the earliest picture in the school, and the next earliest are the others in this room, of which the least important are two unidentified prophets in niches. On the entrance wall on the right, 'Christ before Pilate' is praised as being deeply moving by some critics, condemned as melodramatic by others. In the centre is 'Christ crowned with Thorns, and on the left is 'The Road to Calvary'.

'The Crucifixion' is signed (which is unusual for Tintoretto) and is dated 1565. Its composition is symmetrical but entirely successful. Ruskin declined to comment on it, leaving it, because it is 'beyond all analysis, and above all praise', to 'work its will' on those who see it. But he singled out certain details. He was struck by the figure at the foot of

41 Scuola di San Rocco. Self Portrait by Tintoretto

the Cross, completely covered by a cloak but solid and significant in his view, though it contrasts rather strangely with the other figures drawn and painted in beautiful detail. Also he was moved by the ass in the background eating a palm leaf, into which he read the deepest symbolism, though it is perhaps no more than a fairly simple touch of irony. The man riding the ass is said to be Tintoretto himself. The mounted spectator in a white tunic with a rose-coloured cloak is (so Ruskin says, and it is no doubt so) a portrait of Titian.

With so many hastily or casually painted pictures by Tintoretto, or by him and his assistants, in Venice, this splendid work is a reminder of his magnificent ability to compose and paint when his heart was in his task and he was willing to give enough time to it. He was forty-seven years old when he painted it, mature and technically expert and still inspired by great ambition.

(Also in Index of Artists: Zanchi.)

San Salvatore   R 5

The main structure was designed by Spavento and was built between 1506 and 1534, mainly under the direction of Tullio Lombardo, but the façade is by Sardi, and therefore late 17th century. The interior was finished off by Sansovino, and on the right wall of the nave, beyond a marble statue of the Virgin by Campagna, is his monument to Doge Francesco Venier. The statues on it are by his pupil, Vittoria, that on the left of 'Charity' being partly or wholly a school work and certainly inferior to the bas-relief of the 'Pietà' above and to 'Faith', on the right, which is one of Vittoria's best achievements.

Beyond, on the same wall, is one of Titian's last pictures, an 'Annunciation', painted between 1560 and 1566 and inscribed *Titianus fecit fecit* by way of congratulation to himself on having completed such a labour in his old age. The frame and surround are by Sansovino.

The picture of the 'Transfiguration' on the High Altar was also painted by Titian between these same years. It is pale in colour and most originally have been full of light. It is now somewhat faded and hard to see well, even with the rather feeble illumination that the sacristan will turn on for you. The altar itself is by Guglielmo dei Grigi, but the statue over it is a 16th century addition.

On a few special days in the year the 'Transfiguration' is replaced by a truly splendid silver-gilt reredos, of the first half of the 14th century, slightly added to later. On the central band is the 'Transfiguration' with saints on either side, on the band above the 'Madonna', also flanked by saints, and on the lower one the 'Lamb of Sacrifice' with the symbols of the four Evangelists.

In the chapel that opens off from the left side of the chancel is a picture of 'The Supper at Emmaus' which is often ascribed to Giovanni Bellini, but is credited by Berenson to his follower, Benedetto Diana. This seems much more likely, as the figures are stiff and the objects on the table are set out with a pictorial sense much inferior to Bellini's.

At the chancel end of the left wall of the nave, and so opposite Titian's 'Annunciation', flanking a dull picture are two more statues by Vittoria, of St Roch and St Sebastian, late works, the latter lithe and subtly modelled. The surround of the side door which carries the organ is by Sansovino, and the organ doors are by Titian's brother. The altar next along, with a poor figure of St Jerome on it, is a discreet and tasteful work by Guglielmo dei Grigi.

(Also in Index of Artists: Palma Giovane, Peranda, Piazzetta.)

Gli Scalzi (or Santa Maria di Nazareth)   W Can: 3

The Scalzi are the barefoot Carmelite friars. The church was designed by Longhena, but the Baroque façade is by Giuseppe Sardi. The interior decoration is highly elaborate. The ceiling of the chapel on the right is by Tiepolo, the subject 'St Theresa in Glory', painted when he was young and under the influence of Piazzetta. Two blue glass candlesticks that are often placed on either side of the High Altar are 18th century and from Murano. In the chapel nearest the door on the left side of the nave, on the ceiling is a perished fresco by Tiepolo of 'The Agony in the Garden' with angels all round. Also in this chapel is an exceptionally fine (but rather gruesome) wax representation of 'Christ and the Two Thieves', the origin of which is unknown.

San Sebastiano   WD 3

Designed by Scarpagnino and built over the first half of the 16th century (it is hard to understand why it took more than forty years), this church ranks with the School of San Rocco and the Schiavoni by being entirely and beautifully decorated by Veronese, as they are by Tintoretto and Carpaccio

42   San Sebastiano. 'Esther crowned Queen by Ahasuerus' by Paolo Veronese

respectively. Though he was not more than about thirty when he started to paint these great pictures, all are outstanding for colour and design, for their perfect proportion to their space and setting and for technical skill in linear perspective, which is especially striking in the ceiling paintings. Veronese was also a master of aerial perspective, the absolutely sure relationship, that is, between figures and objects in recession.

On the wall at the end of the right side of the so-called atrium into which you enter there is, very properly, a plaque commemorating the cleaning of all the pictures and the refurbishing of the church generally in 1962 and 1965 at the expense of two sisters called Varzi. Titian's 'St Nicholas of Bari' on the altar on the left of this is weak for him and no doubt largely painted by assistants. Over the first altar on the right wall of the main nave is a picture of the 'Beato Pietro Gambacorti' by Bencovich in the manner of his master,

Piazzetta. Over the third is a late picture of 'The Crucifixion' by Veronese and beyond it is a monument to a Bishop of Cyprus by Sansovino.

Now let us look at the pictures which Veronese painted for the church. The three scenes on the ceiling are from the story of Esther, nearest the door 'Esther led before Ahasuerus', in the centre 'Esther crowned Queen by Ahasuerus', and nearest the altar 'Mordecai (Esther's uncle) carried in Triumph'. The second of these, Ruskin said, was 'remarkable for the light concentrated in the sky in spite of the brilliancy of colour in the figures; it is not merely a white sky, but a beautifully graduated burst of light from behind the canopy of the throne'. On the outside of the organ doors is painted 'The Presentation in the Temple', and on the inside (the sacristan will open or shut them for you) is 'The Pool of Bethesda', both fine works by Veronese. The frieze all round the nave is partly the work of his pupils, but beautifully designed by

43   San Simeone Profeta. 'St Simeon'

him. It disappears into the choir gallery, which is above the door and can be entered by application to the sacristan.

On either side of the chancel are, on the right, 'St Sebastian refusing under Torture to abjure the Faith', and on the left 'St Sebastian [in armour] appearing to St Mark and St Marcellinus and fortifying them in their Martyrdom'. Behind the altar, the 'Virgin in Glory with St Sebastian, St Peter, St John the Baptist, St Catherine and St Francis', and on the arch above and in front of it, 'The Annunciation'.

In the sacristy, which you enter through a passage leading from the left end of the nave, the paintings on the walls are unimportant, except perhaps for the 'Plague of Serpents', which could be by Andrea Schiavone or by Tintoretto when a young man. But on the ceiling the 'Coronation of the Virgin' and four Evangelists are dated 1555 and are the first painted for this church by Veronese.

Back in the main church, in the chapel on the left furthest from the entrance is a youthful picture by Veronese of 'The Virgin and Child with donors'. On the right of it is a charming statue of 'St Antony Abbot' by Vittoria and on the left a weak 'St Mark' by some assistant of his. The grand bust of Marcantonio Grimani on the left wall of this chapel is also by Vittoria. On the corners of the choir screen are four statues by Campagna of the 'Virgin' and 'The Angel of the Annunciation' and two Sybils.

(Also in Index of Artists: Bordone, Palma Giovane.)

Seminario Patriarcale (or di Venezia)
See Pinacoteca Manfrediana

San Silvestro   SP 9
In the first chapel on the right is the 'Baptism of Christ' by Tintoretto. It has recently been cleaned and relieved of some

later additions and is one of the most beautiful Tintorettos in Venice. Ruskin, although he saw it before its successful restoration, greatly admired it, particularly the flow of the stream.* As an example of placing two figures in the area of a picture it is a masterpiece, but it has an intensely moving quality as well.

Opposite it is a rather undistinguished picture in deplorable condition.† But it is of 'San Tomaso Beket', and so the only picture of an English saint in the city. On the left wall also, nearest the door, is a 14th century polyptych, considerably repainted.

San Simeone Profeta (Simeone Grande) SC 4
The facade is modern. In the recently constructed baptistry, which is beyond the first altar on the right wall of the nave, are two early 15th century circular bas-reliefs of 'The Annunciation'. Further along the right wall is an earlier 15th century statue of 'St Valentine', and beyond it a 14th century bas-relief of an 'Abbot worshipping St Simeon'. On the end wall is a delicate half-length angel of about 1400. In the chapel on the left of the chancel there is a magnificent 14th century recumbent figure of 'St Simeon'. The first picture on the left wall of the nave is a 'Last Supper' by Tintoretto, heavily restored.

(Also in Index of Artists: Corona, Mansueti, Palma Giovane.)

Santa Sofia E Can: 3
This church has no facade. Within it there are four 15th century statues in the style of Rizzo, two on the High Altar and two beside the door, of St Luke, St Andrew, St Cosmas and St Damian. On the left wall of the nave is a fine Gothic Madonna, possibly by Bartolomeo Bon.

San Stae (a Venetian abbreviation of S. Eustachio) SC 7
This church, now closed, has an early 18th century facade. In the first chapel on the right of the nave the 'Madonna with St Laurence, St Antony of Padua and St Francis' is by Bambini, and in the third chapel is 'St Oswald in Glory' by Balestra. The ceiling of the chancel has paintings by Sebastiano Ricci. On the right wall of the chancel are, below, 'The Martyrdom of St Bartholomew' by Tiepolo, and the 'Crucifixion of St Andrew' by G.A. Pellegrini, and above, 'St James the Less receiving the Sacrament' by Bambini. On the left wall, below, 'St Jacob bound by a Ruffian' by Piazzetta, 'St Peter escaping from Prison' by Ricci, and the 'Martyrdom of St John the Evangelist' by Balestra. In the chapel nearest the chancel on the left of the nave the Crucifix is by Toretti. In the sacristy is 'St Eustace before Trajan' by Pittoni.

Santo Stefano SM 5
This is a large and ancient church built, in place of an earlier one, in the 14th century and added to in the 15th, but mainly by way of interior decoration. The exterior is thus 14th century and is described by Ruskin as the best ecclesiastical example of 'central Gothic' architecture in Venice. Its 15th century doorway is very beautiful and may be by Bartolomeo Bon, whose style it bears. It is Renaissance-Gothic, like the Porta della Carta (of the Doge's Palace), which it antedates. Ruskin called it first rate, and he much admired 'the manner of the introduction of the figure of the angel at the top of the arch'.

Inside, the church has a glorious 'carena di nave' roof and the typical Venetian 14th century conformation, with two broad aisles separated from the nave by red and white pillars surmounted by frescoed arches. Over the entrance door is a lively wooden equestrian statue of Domenico Contarini, who died in 1650. On the right of the door, as you face it, is a rather dull monument by Vittoria, and next to it, in a niche too high for it to be seen properly, is a lively little early 17th century lively Madonna (out of place, see below). On either side of the second altar on the right wall are two marble statues, one of 'St John the Baptist' by a Lombard sculptor of the 16th century, restored but still very fine, and the other of an allegorical female figure by an unidentified Renaissance sculptor. The bronze bas-relief next to the door into the sacristy, of the 'Virgin with Saints and Donors', is of the date of Leopardi and may be by him.

In the sacristy there are three large pictures by Tintoretto, 'The Last Supper', 'Christ washing the feet of His Disciples' and 'The Agony in the Garden', all fairly late and fairly good, though the last two are somewhat confused. On a chest on the right are two imposing wooden statues of saints, probably removed from the old wooden choir stalls. The statues of 'St Antony' and 'St John the Baptist' on either side of the altar

---

*Nevertheless, describing the stream as an accurate representation of something seen and remembered, he added a wish that Tintoretto had taken the trouble to paint direct from nature.
†It is dated 1520, and is by Girolamo Santacroce, a pupil of Giovanni Bellini. The outer part was painted in the 19th century, and on the rest are beginning to appear those white spots which mean decay.

are late 16th century, and the pictures of 'St Laurence' and 'St Nicholas' (which have been considerably repainted), also on either side of the altar, are by Bartolomeo Vivarini. In the smaller sacristy, which leads off the main one, are two angels on either side of the niche over the door where the 15th century Madonna mentioned above ought to be.

Back in the main church, the chapel on the right of the chancel has three elegant statues, 'The Redeemer', above, and two angels, early 17th century, by Giulio del Moro. In the chancel are, at the sides, the stonework and, behind the High Altar, the woodwork, of the original choir that once stood in the nave. On either side of the High Altar are two large statues of St Mark and St Clare, carved from wood and covered in bronze, by Campagna, and in front of the arch at the top of the screen, marble statues of 'The Madonna' and 'The Angel of the Annunciation', late 16th century and very graceful. The altar front has superb marble inlay.

Coming back along the left wall of the nave you will find over the door of the Baptistry a good Lombardesque statue of 'St Nicholas of Tolentino', and, on the middle altar of the five along the wall, two noble 15th century figures of 'St Paul' and 'St Jerome' by Pietro Lombardo.

(Also in Index of Artists: Bambini, Bordone, Corona, Marieschi, Peranda.)

Go out of the main door of the church, turn right, and over a bridge you are in the Campo S. Angelo. Immediately on your right is the entrance to the cloisters of S. Stefano, late Renaissance, in the style of Scarpagnino and possibly by him. Back in the Campo, on the corner that juts out on the left, is the Oratorio dell' Annunciata, dating from the 12th century. It contains a gilt wood Crucifix, over life-size, of the date of Sansovino, though not by him, and an 'Annunciation' by Palma Giovane with a pitifully weak representation of the Dove in the top right-hand corner.

Beyond, on the left of the Campo is the Palazzo Gritti, and opposite it on the right is the Pallazzo Duodo. Both are 15th century with pointed arches and, on the P. Gritti, coloured marble surrounds, while the P. Duodo is less colourful, brick-built but of fine design, especially the top two storeys.

San Tomà (Now always closed)   **SP 6**
Always so called, though properly S. Tommaso. An unimportant little 18th century church, containing a fresco of the

'Martyrdom of St Thomas' by Jacopo Guarana's son Vincenzo on the ceiling and on the High Altar statues of St Peter and St Thomas by Campagna. Outside on the north wall is a charming bas-relief of the 'Virgin and Monks'.

Two interesting buildings are nearby. Opposite the church in its little campo is the Scuola dei Calegheri (shoemakers), spoilt by the ground-level shop-windows but with a fine door between them and fine windows above. It is late 15th century, and the sculpture on the façade, of St Mark healing a shoemaker, is by Pietro Lombardo.

If you turn right as you leave the church, go just round the corner of it and then left across a bridge, you are in the Calle dei Nomboli and a short way along it on the right (No. 2793) is the Casa Goldoni, a charming 15th century house with a courtyard and open-air staircase therein. It contains relics of Carlo Goldoni, other 18th century theatrical curios and a theatrical library. The façade visible from the bridge curves with the canal. It has typical Venetian window-spacing and, where it was needed functionally, a great chimney protruding from the wall.

Torcello and Burano
The small island of Torcello, some way to the north of Venice, was populated and prosperous before Venice itself. The 7th century circular Baptistry has gone and only a few stones mark its place outside the front of the Cathedral which, with the little church of St Fosca next to it, are the survivors of Torcello's great days. St Fosca was built in the 11th and 12th centuries and is architecturally important and satisfying.

The Cathedral was rebuilt in the 9th century and added to thereafter, particularly in the first years of the 11th. On the south side there are shutters for the windows carved out of stone, hinges and all, in the 11th century. Inside there are many marvellous things. The floor is covered with a form of marble mosaic, and from it rise light-grey columns with Corinthian capitals, all 11th century except the second and third on the right, which are 6th century. The screen, or iconostasis, has 11th century carving of great beauty below and 15th century paintings of the Virgin and the Apostles above. In the chancel are brick seats for the priests in a semi-circle and the bishop's throne in the middle, with the altar in front resting on a Roman sarcophagus carved with youthful figures too pagan to be cherubs.

44   San Trovaso, 'St Chrysogonus' by Giambono

Dominating all, but blending with all, are the mosaics in the chancel apse, in the chapel on the right of the chancel and on the west wall. Taking them in reverse order, those on the west wall represent the 'Last Judgement' in a series of scenes starting with the 'Crucifixion' at the top, then 'Christ descending with his Archangels into Hell', then 'Christ on the Throne of Judgement', then the angels sounding the Resurrection, and finally, in the last two tiers, the souls of the dead sorted into their eternal destinies. These are probably 12th century and have suffered from restorations, but not so as to spoil their general effect. Those in the chapel on the right of the chancel are probably 9th century, and they represent Christ between the Archangels Gabriel and Michael with SS. Augustine, Ambrose, Martin and Gregory below. On the ceiling in front the Mystic Lamb and four angels are probably 12th century. In the chancel apse itself is a superb representation of the Virgin and Child on a gold background, with the twelve Apostles below. The Virgin and Child are 12th or 13th century and the Apostles are 12th, or perhaps 11th, rather heavily repaired and restored but again, like the west wall, not to the point of being spoiled.

Over the altar on the left wall of the nave nearest the west wall is the 'Madonna and the Faithful' by Tintoretto. It is on loan from the Accademia, and Ruskin, who saw it there, called it a 'lovely little Tintoret—purest work of his heart and fairest of his faculty'.

Vaporetti ply fairly frequently between Torcello and Burano, because those on the way out from Venice call at both and those on the way back go from Torcello to Burano and then back to Torcello. The Buranese women and girls are famous for their lace-making and, as you will see, many of the men are fishermen. The restaurants specialize in fish, and the boats give colour to parts of the little island.

Its only works of art are in the church of San Martino and, unless they are moved again, the best, the 'Crucifixion' by Tiepolo, comes first on the left wall. The stout donor in his blue-and-white striped garment is well painted, the rest of the picture hardly less so, but the treatment of the subject shows you how unsuccessful Tiepolo was at coping with divine tragedy.

Behind the High Altar is 'St Mark and other Saints' by Giovanni Bellini's follower Girolamo da Santacroce, the central figure better than the others. In the sacristy* are three pictures by Mansueti, naive as usual (and looking as if

*Not in the oratory of S. Barbara, where they used to be.

they had been revarnished but not cleaned), the 'Marriage of the Virgin', the 'Adoration of the Magi' and the 'Flight into Egypt', which is made rather charming by all the animals escorting the Holy Family.

San Trovaso   ED 1

Though recently restored, this is an undistinguished building, moderately pretty but of no real architectural value, consecrated in 1657. The name is a very strange corruption of SS. Gervasio e Protasio.

Inside there is nothing of any importance in the nave, but from the left transept you can see two pictures by Tintoretto, one of 'The Last Supper' in the chapel that forms the end of the transept, the other of 'The Temptation of St Antony', in the chapel on the left of the chancel. The former, which Ruskin said had been ruined by restoration and was in any case vulgar in conception, is now apparently in good condition and at least shows Tintoretto's painting of detail very well and also his interest in, and conquest of, problems of three-dimensional design. The table is at an angle to the spectator and to the room that it is in. The large figures in the foreground are in shadow and the eye is carried beyond them into the scene.

The 'Temptation of St Antony' is painted in simple tones, like many of Tintoretto's best pictures and, though it is said to have been rather drastically restored, is beautiful and pictorially entirely successful. As an illustration of the sort of temptation that we are told the old saint was put to, including the offer of lust irresistible for an ordinary man, it is either a failure or over-subtle, as the two women, although not fully dressed, are really rather charming and almost demure. The one on the left, whose lure is avarice, is pretty, and the other, who offers carnal sin, 'might', in Ruskin's words, 'be taken for a very respectable person, but that there are flames playing about her loins'.

There are three other pictures to which Tintoretto's name is attached, two of them late and heavy, largely painted by assistants, on either side of the chancel, 'Joachim driven out of the Temple' on the left, and 'The Adoration of the Magi' on the right. The third, 'Christ Washing the Disciples' Feet', which is opposite 'The Last Supper' in the left transept, is probably entirely a school picture with nothing in it by Tintoretto's own hand.

In the right transept, on the end wall beside the door is a very good and early (15th century) picture of 'St Chryso-

45 San Zaccaria. The 'Adoration of the Magi' by Bambini

gonus on a Horse', by Michele Giambono. The Clary chapel on the right of it has an altar on the front of which is a lovely bas-relief of an angel choir by an unidentified 15th century sculptor of this type of Pietro Lombardo.

(Also in Index of Artists: Marconi, Palma Giovane, Domenico Tintoretto.)

Opposite the east door, across the canal, is the dignified 15th century Palazzo Nani-Barbarigo, with ogee windows and a coat of arms.

San Vitale   **SM 4**

The present building was erected around 1700 and is in a rather heavy Palladian style. It is no longer used as a church and the method of getting into it has changed frequently. The present method is simple. You go in by the main door and pay 100 lire to a Catholic Society (the Unione Cattolica artisti italiani), and the attendant who takes your money will turn on some good lighting for the three principal pictures.

On the right at the far end of the nave is one of them, by Piazzetta, beautifully composed and painted in muffled tones. The foreground figure of a monk could hardly be bettered, given Piazzetta's method, date and school. The monk is St Antony of Padua, and the other saint, below the Archangel Raphael, is St Louis.

Over the altar is a bold, well-preserved picture by Carpaccio, painted in his old age, the central figure being St Vitale on a white horse, between St John the Baptist, St George, St James and St Valeria. The Virgin and Child are above the parapet. On a part of the arch to the left there is a small green parrot.

In front of the picture are two rather humdrum 18th century statues by a sculptor called Gai, only worth noting because of the rather felicitous way in which the veil over the face of Faith (or is it Fortitude?) on the left is represented.

On the left, opposite the Piazzetta, is a good example of the work of Sebastiano Ricci. The subject is the 'Immaculate Conception of the Virgin Mary'. The blue and white robes are pretty enough, but there is not a grain of religion, tenderness or feeling in the picture, and not very much artistic merit.

Next to this is a strong, competent 'Crucifixion' by Piazzetta's pupil, Giulia Lama. Then comes 'St Sebastian and Joseph and St Frances of Paola, by Pellegrini, opposite it.

112

Across the campo lurks the Palazzo Pisani, built at the turn of the 17th century. 'Late Renaissance, and of no merit', says Ruskin, 'but grand in its colossal proportions...' The interior courtyard may please you more than either facade.

San Zaccaria — W Cas: 9

The first architect of this church was Antonio Gambello, who designed it on Gothic lines and supervised its building from 1444 to 1465. It was then taken over by Mauro Coducci, who about 1500 gave it its remarkable façade, Venetian Renaissance strongly influenced by Venetian Gothic. Inside, the Gothic start and the Renaissance finish are not merged at all but stand side by side or the latter on top of the former, producing a strange but by no means unpleasant result.

The figure of 'St Zacharias' over the main door is by Vittoria, as also are the fine figures of 'St John the Baptist' and 'St Zacharias' just inside on the holy-water stoups. In the main church the one great picture is Giovanni Bellini's 'Madonna and Saints', the second on the left wall of the nave (it used to be the first and that is where most guide-books put it), damaged and too often badly restored, but finally carefully cleaned and restored again in 1971. It is a marvellous achievement of Bellini's old age. The saints are Peter, Catherine, Lucy and Jerome, who is reading a book.

It was painted in 1505, when Bellini was about seventy-four years of age and, as Albrecht Dürer said on a visit to Venice in that year, 'very old and still the best in painting'. Giorgione's 'Castelfranco Madonna' had been finished in the previous year, and some of the young man's influence can be seen, principally in the modelling of the heads of the four saints. But not in the skill with which the harmony of the picture is accomplished. In the combination of accurate drawing in perspective and the lapping of every figure and object with accurately observed light, so that every part stands clear in its own spatial ambience and is perfectly related to the rest, Bellini is seen to be a master of what he had taught himself. He has unerringly planned the whole picture-space in three dimensions. The light holds the group together without ever marring the local colour, and, like St Benedict in the Frari triptych, St Peter and St Jerome, turning towards us, free the composition from formality and, as it were, draw us in.

At the end of this wall of the nave is a monument to Vittoria, begun by him himself and finished by a relation. On the right of the nave is a huge 'Adoration of Magi' by Nicolò Bambini, which has recently been cleaned, like the Bellini. The 'Adoration of the Shepherds' beyond the second altar is also by him or perhaps by Balestra. In the large lunettes high up are seven recently restored pictures by (R to L) Zanchi (entrance wall), Bambini, Fumiani (two), right wall, and left wall Zanchi, Andrea Celesti (two), mostly subjects to do with the church. In the right-hand chapel behind the chancel is a good picture of 'St Peter in Prayer' with a cock, by Francesco Rosa (Neapolitan, 17th century).

In the chapel of S. Anastasio, the entry to which is at the end of the right transept, there is a Crucifixion attributed to Van Dyck and also a poor early picture by Tintoretto, of 'The Birth of St John the Baptist'. In the chapel of S. Tarasio, which leads off it, there are frescoes on the ceiling by Andrea del Castagno, one of the best Florentine painters in the gap between Masaccio and the outburst of the full Renaissance. They are of Evangelists and other Saints, and a band of very Florentine putti forms their hither edge. There is a second signature to them, that of Francesco of Faenza, but there is little doubt that they were mainly painted by Andrea del Castagno, who is known to have visited Venice when a young man, and they are accordingly the first early Renaissance paintings in the city. There are also three polyptychs in magnificent gilded and decorated frames that are themselves signed by their maker, Ludovico da Forli. The pictures in them are all by Antonio Vivarini and his partner Giovanni d'Alemagna, and were painted in 1443 (the date is on the frames), except for the three in the centre of the one on the altar, which are signed 'Stefano Plebanus di S. Agnese 1385'. On the back of this are some damaged and faded figures, the top row by Vivarini and d'Alemagna, the lower row probably by 'Stefano'.

(Also in Index of Artists: Fumiani, Palma Giovane, Strozzi, Domenico Tiepolo.)

If you leave the church and cross the Campo to the right-hand corner, you will pass under an arch with a relief of the Virgin and Child on the far side, 15th century but of no great merit. Turn right into the Calle S. Provolo which leads into the Fondamenta dell'Osmarin and on your left, across the canal, you will see the Palazzo Priuli, one of the finest secular buildings in Venice. It is Venetian Gothic, completed before 1450, and, says Ruskin, 'a most important and beautiful early Gothic palace' with very early windows in the lower storey and a beautiful range of windows above. He thinks that the splendid traceried angle-windows are rather later, but they marvellously complete the façade and solve its turns to the side walls, that on the left being the more delicate of the two.

San Zulian (always so called, though properly San Giuliano)
SM 13

This church was reconstructed in 1553-5 by Sansovino and Vittoria at the expense of an unconventional but successful doctor called Tommaso Rangone. Over the main door in the façade, which is Sansovino's, there is a fine bronze statue of the doctor by him, nearly always covered with pigeon droppings.

Inside, on the entrance wall are 'St Roch and the Sick' and the 'Death of St Roch' by Sante Peranda, both on the right of the handsome organ loft, as you face it. The first picture on the right wall at the normal level, of the 'Pietà with Three Saints', by Paolo Veronese (though Berenson does not mention it), may have been a noble one but has been ruined, especially the lower part, by restoration. The next picture, over a pediment, of 'St Jerome', competent but dull, is by Leandro Bassano. On the next altar the statues of 'St Daniel' and 'St Catherine' and the bas-relief on the front, of the 'Birth of the Virgin', are by Vittoria. Over this altar and in the chapel on the right of the chancel are weak pictures by Palma Giovane, and his too is the rather better picture in the centre of the ceiling, the subject of which is 'St Julian in Glory'.

The two pictures in the chancel, one on either side, of 'A Miracle of St Julian' and 'The Martyrdom of St Julian', late 17th century, are by Antonio Zanchi and are not too bad of their kind. The lunette on the right wall of the chapel on the left of the chancel, depicting the 'Fall of Manna', is by Leonardo Corona, and on the altar here are a marble alto-relievo of 'Christ supported by Angels' in the centre, and figures of 'The Madonna' and 'St Mary Magdalene' on either side, by Campagna. These two figures are of terracotta painted, unsuccessfully, to look like bronze.

5 Summary Notes on Other Churches

S. Agnese
Rebuilt about 1850. For entry, ask at Dorsoduro, No. 898.

Not on map. ED near Gesuati

S. Anna
Built 1634–59. Now part of a sailors' hospital.

E. Cas: 3

S. Biagio
Early 18th century. Always closed, with the Naval Museum next to it. (See Index of Artists: Canova.)

E. Cas: 1

S. Canciano
Early 18th century façade. Two pictures by Zanchi in the chancel (ruinous).

E. Can: 5

Cappucine
Early 17th century. Over the door, a late 16th century relief of the Madonna, probably by Campagna.

Not on map. W. Can: near Ghetto Nuovo

S. Caterina
Closed always. The good pictures that were once inside have been removed.

Not on map. E. Can: near Gesuiti

Oratorio dei Catecumeni
Altar-piece by Leandro Bassano.

Not on map. ED adjoining Spirito Santo

S. Giovanni dei Cavalieri di Malta
In the chancel are arms of the Knights of Malta and of the Prior of the Order.

W. Cas: 14

S. Giovanni Novo
Built in 1762 in Palladian style. Open Sundays. Contains an early polychrome crucifix.

W. Cas: 8

S. Gregorio
Closed and used by the Belle Arti for restoration of pictures. A fine 14th century Gothic façade and beautiful cloisters, built in 1342.

ED 6

The Maddalena
Late 18th century, circular outside, hexagonal inside. Open Sundays, for Mass.

W. Can: 8

S. Maria Maggiore
Used as a warehouse. Unimpressive 16th century façade.

Not on map. WD near gasometer

S. Maria dei Penitenti
Seldom open. 17th century. **Façade** unfinished. Interior attractive. Chancel arch and ceiling painted by Marieschi with putti and the 'Apotheosis of St Laurence Giustiniani'.

W. Can: 1

S. Maria del Pianto or **delle Cappucine**
Probably by Longhena. **Façade** elegantly curved. Now a school and invisible behind a high wall.

W. Cas: 5

S. Maria dei Servi
Private. Gothic door of adjoining convent remains.

Not on map. W. Can near S. Marziale

S. Maria della Visitazione   E.D. 3
(or **S. Girolamo dei Gesuati**)
Present building is early 16th century.
Fine facade. Tuscan decoration inside.

S. Maurizio   SM 6
Rebuilt in 1806.

Nome di Gesù or **S. Chiara**   Not on map. SC
Early 19th century.   near S. Andrea

Ognissanti   Not on map. WD
Early 16th century Renaissance. Very   near S. Trovaso
plain. Not open to the public and con-
tains nothing worth seeing.

S. Samuele   SM 3
Mostly late 17th century. Contains 'Crucifixion' by Domenico Veneziano. Only
used for weddings.

SS. Simeone e Giuda (Simeone Piccolo)   SC 3
Early 18th century. Noted for its truly
hideous dome. Permanently closed.

Spirito Santo   ED 5
Early 16th century Lombardesque
façade. Open Sunday mornings, and contains pictures by Guarana and Palma
Giovane.

S. Teresa   Not on map. WD
17th century with early 18th century   near S. Nicolò
façade. Fine 17th century High Altar.
Permanently closed. Said to have a picture by Guarana.

The Zitelle (properly **Santa Maria della**   G 3
Presentazione or **delle Zitelle**)
An unattractive little building by a fol-
lower of Palladio. The 'Agony in the
Garden' on the right wall is by Palma
Giovane. Permanently closed.

6 The Grand Canal

There are so many buildings along the Grand Canal that it is useful for a start to be able to identify and locate some of the best and most easily recognizable of them. The list that follows includes the principal High Renaissance and later palaces, several notable earlier buildings, two freaks and three impostors. Their positions are related to some of the vaporetto stations, the names of which are clearly painted on them, and they are grouped within four main 'reaches' bounded by the Salute, the Accademia and its bridge, the main bend of the Canal (right-handed as you go in this direction), the Rialto Bridge and the railway station.

But first a word about the bridges. The Accademia Bridge was built in 1932 and was intended to be temporary. But as it is quite pretty and unpretentious, and everyone has come to like it, it will probably remain as long as it will last, and it has in fact recently been repaired and reinforced. The Rialto Bridge was built at the end of the 16th century. It is not particularly beautiful but is reasonably picturesque. Its chief architect was appropriately called Antonio da Ponte.

As you enter the Canal from the open Bacino, there stands, at the point on the left, the Dogana or Customs House. The wind-vane on the sphere, which is supported by two Atlas-like figures, is of fickle Fortune, 17th century, by a sculptor called Giuseppe Benoni.

First Reach, Salute to Accademia
1. On the right, just beyond Sta. Maria del Giglio vaporetto station, the Palazzo Corner, by Sansovino, late 16th century, now the prefecture of police.

2. On the left, opposite, the small very beautiful early Renaissance Palazzo Dario, late 15th century, possibly, but probably not, by Pietro Lombardo (Plate 46).

3. Next but one to it, in a garden, the one-storey Palazzo Guggenheim, which contains Miss Guggenheim's collection of modern art. The local equivalent of the law of 'ancient lights' stopped the building when it had only got as far as this, and left it a conspicuous freak.

4. On the right, the last building, a large one, before the Accademia Bridge, the Palazzo Franchetti. Though part of it is 15th century, this palace was restored and added to at the end of the 19th century and has to count as one of the 'impostors'.

Second Reach, Accademia to the main bend
5. On the right, a short way beyond the bridge, an even more abortive freak than the Palazzo Guggenheim, in the form of a grand palace of which only a pillar or two and a bit of rustic wall remain. Above them is an ordinary house.

6. On the left, at the Cà Rezzonico vaporetto station, a small hopelessly overdone fake-early-Renaissance edifice, the second 'impostor'.

7. Next beyond it, the large Palazzo Rezzonico, late High Renaissance, by Longhena, mid 17th century (Plate 48). This contains a permanent exhibition of 18th century furniture and minor pictures. Here Robert Browning lived and died.

8. Opposite, on the right, the Palazzo Grassi, by Giorgio Massari, perhaps the principal 18th century classical secular building in Venice. It now houses a collection of costumes and is used for special exhibitions.

9. On the left, the first of three all together just before the wide side canal that leads off at the main bend of the Grand Canal, one of the pair of Palazzi Giustiniani.

10. Next to it the other Palazzo Giustiniani (Plate 48). These two were started in the 15th century, but have been altered since. Wagner lived here in the 1850s.

46　Grand Canal. Palazzo Dario

47   Grand Canal, Palazzo Pesaro

11. Next to the Palazzo Foscari (Plate 48), right on the corner, a Venetian-Gothic palace equally grand and also mid 15th century.

Third Reach, main bend to Rialto Bridge
12. On the right, just beyond the S. Angelo vaporetto station, the Palazzo Corner-Spinelli, about 1500, by Coducci, Renaissance but pleasantly Venetian.
13. Farther along on the right, standing high above the neighbouring buildings, and with a grand classical façade, the Palazzo Grimani, designed and partly built by Sanmicheli in the first half of the 16th century and finished after his death.

Now occupied by the court of appeal. The two statues of 'Victory' on the entrance arch are by Vittoria.

14. On the left, opposite the Palazzo Grimani, the Palazzo Coccina-Tiepolo-Papadopoli, mid 16th century, by Giacomo, son of Guglielmo dei Grigi, well proportioned, with two pinnacles aloft.

Fourth Reach, Rialto Bridge to the railway station
15. Just through the bridge on the left, the Palazzo dei Camerlenghi, early 16th century by the Lombard architect called Guglielmo dei Grigi Bergamasco. And on the right the

48   Grand Canal. Palazzi Rezzonico, Guistiniani and Foscari

Fondaco dei Tedeschi, by Spavento and Scarpagnino, now the main Post Office.

16. Farther on, on the right, at the vaporetto station that bears its name, the Cà d'Oro, early 15th century and the most famous Venetian-Gothic building on the canal. Its name derives from the fact that much of the façade originally was gilded. It now contains a collection of pictures, only a few of them good, objets d'art, including some fine bronzes and medallions, and furniture.

17. On the left, about halfway to the next vaporetto station (San Stae), the Palazzo Pesaro (now the gallery of modern art and oriental art), started in the 1670s by Longhena and finished after his death in 1682 (Plate 47). A massive late High Renaissance building.

18. On the right, beyond the San Stae vaporetto station, the Palazzo Vendramin-Calergi, a masterpiece of Venetian Renaissance architecture designed by Coducci, started towards the end of the 15th century and finished in 1509, Coducci having died in 1504. It is used as a Casino early and late in the year.

19. On the left, just farther on, the Fondaco dei Turchi, which was almost entirely rebuilt in the 19th century, and so, though it is in the style of the original early Venetian-Gothic building and incorporates some of its materials, must be classed as another 'impostor'.

(Also in Index of Artists: Aspetti, Sanmicheli, Sardi, Scarpagnino.)

You are strongly recommended to get to know these buildings first, because, even though some of them are unimportant, they are reasonably conspicuous and reasonably evenly spaced, and the worst way of dealing with the Grand Canal is to go along it trying to identify building after building, to the right and to the left. This following list is the 'fill-in' which you are advised to keep until you are familiar with the first one.

First Reach

Palazzo Giustinian. R.	Just beyond the Hotel Monaco and so before you are even opposite the Dogana. Gothic, late 15th century, but restored.
P. Contarini Fasan. R.	Dead opposite the Salute. Ruskin said that this 15th century building, sometimes called the 'House of Desdemona', showed 'how much beauty and dignity may be bestowed on a very small and unimportant dwelling-house by Gothic sculpture'.
San Gregorio. L.	In the building next beyond the Salute the pretty door and windows are remains of the 14th century abbey of S. Gregorio.
Hotel Gritti. R.	Early 15th century, but much restored.
P. Contarini dal Zaffo. L.	Next but one before Accademia. Very fine 15th century Venetian Renaissance.

Second Reach

P. Giustinian Lolin. R.	Whitish, with two pinnacles, first detached building beyond Accademia Bridge. Ruskin called it 'of no importance' but it is by Longhena.
P. Falier. R.	Next after P. Giustinian Lolin (and next before the 'most abortive freak', No. 5 in the first list). 15th century Gothic with original open loggias.
P. Contarini degli Scrigni and P. Corfu. L.	Opposite P. Falier. The former, 17th century by Scamozzi, fairly unsuccessfully carries out the lines of the latter, which is 15th century, rather spoilt by later modifications.
P. Loredan dell'Ambasciatore. L.	A tall building, next but one to the P. Corfu. Well-proportioned early 15th century Gothic, but the two figures in alcoves are later 15th century additions.
S. Samuele's campanile. R.	Mostly visible above a small modern building behind S. Samuele vaporetto station. 12th century.

Third Reach

P. Balbi. L.	First beyond 'main bend', with two pinnacles. 'Of no importance' says Ruskin, but imposing and perhaps by Vittoria.

P. Contarini delle Figure. R.	Opposite P. Balbi. 16th century Renaissance, associating, according to Ruskin 'Byzantine .principles of colour with the severest lines of the Roman pediment'. Probably by Scarpagnino.	*Fourth Reach* Fabbriche Vecchie and Fabbriche Nuove. L.	Markets beyond P. dei Camerlenghi. The former early 16th century by Scarpagnino, the latter mid 16th century by Sansovino, by no means a masterpiece of this great architect.
P. Pisani-Moretta. L.	The Rio di S. Polo is opposite the S. Angelo vaporetto station and just before it is this fine 15th century Gothic palazzo, restored, but not too badly, early in the 16th century.	Cà da Mosto. R.	Largest building in group opposite Fabbriche Nuove. 13th century, but much restored.
P. Bernardo. L.	On the corner of the next small Rio. 'A very noble pile of early 15th century Gothic, founded on the Ducal Palace.' (Ruskin).	P. Corner della Regina. L.	Third before P. Pesaro, and as big. 18th century, classical, imposing.
P. Corner-Contarini dei Cavalli. R.	Next before P. Grimani. Restored, but original fine 15th century windows remain.	P. Belloni-Battaggia. L.	Next but one before Fondaco dei Turchi (the building between being the 15th century granary). By Longhena in his Baroque style, surmounted by yet another pair of pinnacles.
P. Dolfin-Manin. R.	Standing alone just before the Rialto vaporetto station. By Sansovino, 16th century. Now Banca d'Italia.		

7 Palaces and Other Buildings not on the Grand Canal

The following are to be found under their own names: Arsenale, Bovolo, Scuola di S. Giovanni Evangelista, Palazzo Labia, Scuola di San Marco, Ospedaletto.

The following are mentioned under the churches etc. nearest to them:

Annunciata, Oratorio dell': S. Stefano
Palazzo Ariani: Angelo Raffaelle
Ateneo Veneto: S. Fantino
P. Bernardo: S. Polo
P. Bon: S. Maria Formosa
Calegheri, Scuola dei: S. Toma
P. Corner-Mocenigo: S. Polo
P. Doria: S. Maria Formosa
P. Duodo: S. Stefano
P. Fortuny, *see* P. Pesaro
P. Giustiniani-Faccanon: S. Maria della Fava
Casa Goldoni: S. Toma
P. Grimani: S. Maria Formosa
P. Gritti: S. Stefano
P. Gussoni: S. Lio
P. Malipiero-Trevisan: S. Maria Formosa
S. Margherita, buildings in Campo: S. Maria del Carmine, School
P. Nani-Barbarigo: S. Trovaso
P. Orfei, *see* P. Pesaro
P. Pesaro, *or* degli Orfei, *or* Fortuny: S. Benedetto
P. Pisani: S. Vitale
P. Priuli: S. Zaccaria
Salvadego, Albergo del: Museo Correr
P. Soranzo: S. Maria dei Miracoli
Varotari, Scuola dei: S. Maria del Carmine, School
P. Vitturi: S. Maria Formosa
P. Zenobio: S. Maria del Carmelo, Church
P. Zorzi (Coducci): S. Maria Formosa
P. Zorzi (old): S. Giorgio dei Greci

Index of Artists

This index covers the works in Venice of many artists and of the principal architects and sculptors, whether they are in the main part of the Guide or not. For any work that is in the main part only the reference is the name of the church, gallery or other building concerned, but for those that are not in it enough details are given to make it easy to locate and identify them.

In explanation of the directions, 'R' and 'L' stand for right and left respectively, 'N' stands for Nave (wall of), 'T' for Transept, 'e.w.' for entrance wall, 'ch.' for chapel, and 'Ch.' for Chancel. Thus, for example, '3RN' means the third altar, chapel or major picture on the right wall of the nave, and '2LN' means the second on the left wall, but coming back from the chancel end. 'LT' means left transept, 'ch. R of Ch.' means the chapel on the right of the chancel, and 'e.w.L.' means the left of the entrance wall as you look at it from inside the church. 'S.' stands for 'San', 'Santa', etc. and 'SS.' for Santi, but in the Doge's Palace 'S.d.' means 'Sala di', 'Sala dello', etc. 'P' stands for 'Palazzo'.

PAINTERS
There are seven painters who require more than just a list, Giovanni Bellini, Carpaccio, Giorgione, Titian, Tintoretto, Paolo Veronese and Tiepolo.

Giovanni Bellini (c. 1430 to 1516)
There are three marvellous pictures by Giovanni Bellini in Venice, the triptych in the sacristy of the Frari of the 'Madonna with Four Saints', 'St Jerome with St Christopher and St Augustine' (a late rather Giorgionesque picture) in S. Giovanni Crisostomo, and the 'Madonna with Four Saints' in S. Zaccaria, which has recently (1971) been cleaned. He is very well represented also in the Accademia, and one of the two pictures in S. Pietro Martire at Murano, the 'Virgin and Child with St Augustine, St Mark and a Doge', is a mature masterpiece. The 'Virgin and Child' in the church of the Madonna dell'Orto is charming, and the 'Virgin and Saints' in S. Francesco della Vigna is pleasant and colourful, though marred by the painted-in figure of the donor. There are also pictures by him in the Doge's Palace, in the Museo Correr, in SS. Giovanni e Paolo (a polyptych), and in the Querini-Stampalia Gallery. The 'Supper at Emmaus' in S. Salvatore is ascribed to him by some, and the 'Madonna with a Palm-Tree' in the Cà d'Oro is attributed to him by Berenson against all probability.

Carpaccio, Vittore (1465 to 1525)
Vittore Carpaccio is represented magnificently by the nine paintings that decorate the Scuola di S. Giorgio degli Schiavoni, and by the other nine in the Accademia that illustrate the life and death of St Ursula. In the Accademia there are three other good pictures by him, the S. Giobbe altar-piece in *Room II* depicting the 'Presentation', the canal scene in *Room XX,* and the tender 'Meeting of Joachim and Anna' in the corridor called *Room XIX.* There is also a 'Martyrdom of the Ten Thousand' in *Room II,* which is, to borrow an apt phrase from Ruskin, 'journeyman's work', and in *Room XIX* a curious picture of a vision.

Besides these, not to be missed are his 'Two Courtesans' in the Correr Museum (where there are also a 'Visitation' and a portrait, neither of which may be by him, and a predella panel of 'St Peter Martyr', the 'St George and the Dragon' in S. Giorgio Maggiore and 'St Vidal on Horseback with other Saints' in S. Vitale. His 'Lion of St Mark' in the Ducal Palace is the finest lion of its kind, and that completes the list, unless you go to Chioggia and see the recently restored 'St Paul' in the church of S. Domenico there, or unless you think that Carpaccio had any hand in the two feeble pictures in the Cà d'Oro that are ascribed to him.

Giorgione (c. 1478 to 1510)

There are only two pictures in Venice by Giorgione, both in the Accademia, the superb 'Tempesta' and 'La Vecchia', unless the cassone panel of 'Apollo and Daphne' in the Pinacoteca Manfrediana is by him or 'Christ Carrying the Cross' in the Scuola di S. Rocco, which also is ascribed to him by Berenson. But Castelfranco is well within reach of Venice and worth a visit to see there his lovely 'Madonna enthroned with St Francis and St Liberale'.

Titian, or in full Tiziano Vecellio (1488 to 1576)

Titian had a long life and painted until the end of it. He was very highly regarded in his lifetime, and has been so ever since all over Europe, and latterly all over the Western world. Therefore many of his works that were originally in Venice have found their way elsewhere. Moreover he was commissioned by Charles V and Philip II of Spain, and most of what he painted for them is in the Prado in Madrid, or in other cities where they held court.

The two best pictures by him in Venice are the 'Assumption' and the 'Pesaro Madonna' in the Frari. In spite of Ruskin's disapproval, most critics think highly of his altar-piece of 'St Mark and other Saints' and his ceiling paintings in the sacristy of the Salute. There is also a 'Descent of the Holy Spirit' by him in the main part of that church. In the Accademia the 'Pietà', painted in his old age to be an altar-piece for his own tomb, is far better than the carefully executed but bathetic 'Portrait of a Man as John the Baptist', and the 'Presentation', which Ruskin found fault with, is no mean accomplishment.

'St Laurence' in the Gesuiti, 'St John' in S. Giovanni Elemosinario, the 'Sapienza' in the Libreria and 'St Christopher' and the 'Doge Grimani and Faith', both in the Ducal Palace, the 'Annunciation' and 'Transfiguration' in S. Salvatore and other 'Annunciation' in the Scuola di S. Rocco are all distinguished. 'St Nicholas of Bari' in S. Sebastiano, probably partly a school picture, 'St James of Compostella' in S. Lio, which is in a sad condition, 'Tobias and the Angel' in S. Marziale and the 'Dead Christ' in the Scuola di S. Rocco make up the rest of the list, as the 'Infant Christ and two Saints' in S. Marcuola is now generally agreed not to be by Titian.

Tintoretto, Jacopo Robusti, called (1518 to 1594)

Tintoretto presents the problem of being prolifically repre-sented all over the city. There are fine and famous pictures by him in the school and church of San Rocco, in the Doge's Palace, in the Accademia, S. Giorgio Maggiore, the Salute and the Madonna dell'Orto. But the list of places where he is to be found is formidable, and the rest are as follows: Libreria Marciana, S. Cassiano, Museo Correr, S. Felice, the Gesuati, the Gesuiti, S. Giuseppe in Castello, S. Lazzaro dei Mendicanti, S. Maria Mater Domini, S. Maria Zobenigo, S. Marziale, S. Moisè, S. Polo, S. Silvestro, S. Simeone Grande, S. Stefano, Torcello, S. Trovaso and S. Zaccaria.

The greatest and best-known of Tintoretto's pictures in Venice are, as indicated above, the 'Crucifixion' in the Scuola di S. Rocco (and some others there), the 'Paradiso' and 'Bacchus and Ariadne' (and the other three in the Ante-Collegio) in the Doge's Palace, the 'Miracle of St Mark' in the Accademia and the 'Presentation' in the Madonna dell'Orto. There are many others that are nearly of this class in general esteem, such as the 'Last Judgement' and the 'Golden Calf' also in the Madonna dell'Orto, the 'Madonna dei Camerlenghi' in the Accademia, the 'Feast in Cana' in the Salute, and one or two 'Last Suppers', and large biblical scenes in S. Giorgio Maggiore and elsewhere. But some, less well known, that are of great quality and great beauty are the self-portrait in the Scuola di S. Rocco, 'Adam and Eve' and 'Cain and Abel' and the other pair, 'St George and St Louis' and 'St Andrew and St Jerome', hung next to them in the Accademia, the portrait of Doge Morosini there, the 'Baptism of Christ' in S. Silvestro, and, less fine perhaps, but full of charm, the 'Temptation of St Antony' in S. Trovaso.

Paolo Veronese, Paolo Caliari, called (c. 1528 to 1588)

For Paolo Veronese S. Sebastiano is a treasure-house, and in the Accademia are the 'Feast in the House of Levi' and twenty other pictures of various merit. If you also see his splendid ceilings and wall-paintings in the Doge's Palace, you will have done him justice. But other pictures by him are in the Libreria Marciana, SS. Giovanni e Paolo, S. Luca, S. Pantaleone, S. Pietro di Castello, S. Polo and S. Pietro Martire at Murano.

Tiepolo, Giovanni Battista (1696 to 1770)

A Tiepolo tour in Venice is strongly recommended because he (I mean Giovanni Battista Tiepolo, not his son, Giovanni Domenico, who is treated by one quite well-known guide-book as being the same person) is to be found in pleasant places and variously successful in various moods. Perhaps one day the Palazzo Labia will be open to the public officially, but, if you ask, you are almost sure to be allowed in. If not, there is no better start for a Tiepolo tour than the Scuola del Carmine, where he is at his decorative best.

Two of his most successful pictures are the 'Communion of St Lucy' in SS. Apostoli and the 'Virgin as a Child with St Anne and St Joachim' in S. Maria della Fava. Ambitious failures, but well worth seeing, are the three in S. Alvise. There are good ceiling paintings in the Pietà, and a good picture, as well as good ceiling paintings, in the Gesuati. The four ceilings in the Cà Rezzonico are worth a visit, and are better by far than the popular 'pagliacci' decorations there by Domenico Tiepolo. In the Doge's Palace is Giambattista's excellent 'Neptune offering the riches of the sea to Venice'.

Tiepolo is also to be found in the Accademia (Rooms XI, XV, XVI and XVII), S. Benedetto, Gli Scalzi, S. Francesco della Vigna, S. Stae (if it is reopened), the Ospedaletto, S. Polo, the Scuola di S. Rocco, the Querini-Stampalia gallery and S. Martino on Burano. To keep this guide to reasonable limits, some of the islands which hardly repay visits are not included. Let it be said however that there is a good early Tiepolo on a ceiling in the chiesetta on S. Lazzaro degli Armeni.

d'Alemagna, Giovanni (c. 1400-1450)
Accademia, Room XXIV,
S. Pantaleone
S. Zaccaria

Antonello da Messina (1430-1479)
Museo Correr, Room 11, and see Chapter 2.

Balestra, Antonio (1666-1740)
S. Bartolomeo
S. Cassiano
Gesuiti
Scuola di S. Maria del Carmine, side room on upper floor, 'Rest on the Flight into Egypt'
S. Marziale
S. Pantaleone e.w.r., 'Raising of Lazarus'
S. Stae
S. Zaccaria

Bambini, Nicolò (1651-1736)
Doge's Palace:
    S.d. Quattro Porte, over courtyard windows, 'Venice leaning on the World'
    S.d. Scrutinio, 'Doge Michiel refusing Lordship of Sicily'
Palazzo Patriarcale, ceremonial hall, 'Time revealing Virtue' and 'Virtue driving away Vices'
Galleria d'Arte Moderna, P. Pesaro
Frari, LT, above door, 'Massacre of the Innocents'
S. Marcuola, in adjacent Oratory of Crucifix, 'Deposition'
Scuola di S. Maria del Carmine, lower hall, monochromes
S. Moisè
S. Pantaleone
S. Stae
S. Stefano, 1RN, 'Birth of the Virgin'
S. Zaccaria

Basaiti, Marco (c. 1470-1535)
Accademia, Rooms II and XIX
S. Pietro di Castello

Bassano, Jacopo da Ponte, called (1510-1592)
Doge's Palace: Ante-Collegio
Accademia, Room XIII
S. Cassiano
S. Giorgio Maggiore

Bastiani, Lazzaro (1430-1512)
Accademia, Room XX, 'Reception of the Relic'
S. Antonino
Museo Correr, Room V
Murano, SS. Maria e Donato
Redentore, sacristy, 'Madonna in Worship and Child'

Bellini, Gentile (1429-1507)
Accademia, Rooms XX and XXIII
Capella di S. Basso
Museo Correr, Room 13

Bellini, Giovanni
See above

Bellini, Jacopo (c. 1400-1470)
Accademia, Room IV
Museo Correr, Room 13

Bissolo, Francesco (C. 1465-1554)
Accademia, Room XIX
S. Giovanni in Bragora, Chapel L of Ch., triptych of 'St Andrew, St Jerome and St Martin' S. Maria Mater Domini
S. Maria Mater Domini

Bonifazio
See Pitati

Bordone, Paris (1500-1571)
Accademia, Room VI
Cà d'Oro, Room II, 'Venus Asleep'
S. Giobbe
S. Giovanni in Bragora, Ch., 'Last Supper'
Galleria Querini Stampalia, Room IX
S. Stefano, sacristy, 'Baptism of Christ'

Botticini, Francesco (1446-1492)
Cà d'Oro, Room IV

Canaletto, Antonio (1697-1768)
Accademia, Room XVII

Carpaccio
See above

Castagno, Andrea del (c. 1420-1457)
S. Zaccaria

Catena, Vincenzo (1470-1531)
Accademia, Room III, 'St Bonaventure, St Francis and St Louis'*
S. Maria Formosa
S. Maria Mater Domini
Galleria Querini-Stampalia, Room IX

Cima da Conegliano, Giambattista (1459-1517)
Accademia, Rooms Rooms II, III and XXIII
Cà d'Oro, Room X
Mueso Correr, Room 14
S. Giovanni in Bragora
The Madonna dell'Orto
Pinacoteca Manfrediana, Room 1
S. Maria del Carmelo

*In Catalogue and Guide, but recently not on view.

Corona, Leonardo (1561-1605)
S. Bartolomeo
S. Fantino
S. Giovanni Elemosinario
Murano, Glass Museum
S. Nicolò dei Mendicoli
S. Simeone Profeta, 3LN, 'Visitation'
S. Stefano, 5LN, 'Madonna and Saints'
S. Zulian

Credi, Lorenzo di (1459-1537)
Galleria Querini-Stampalia, Room VIII

Crivelli, Carlo (1430-1495)
Accademia, Room XXIII, parts of altar-piece, 'St Jerome and St Augustine', 'St Peter and St Paul'

Diana, Benedetto (c. 1460-1525)
Accademia, Room XX, 'Miracle of the True Cross'
Cà d'Oro, Room XI, the 'Virgin between St Francis and St Jerome, and two Worshippers'
S. Salvatore

Fumiani, Giovanni Antonio (1643-1710)
S. Benedetto, 2LN, the 'Virgin and Saints'
Gesuiti, sacristy ceiling, monochromes of the 'Four Evangelists'
S. Pantaleone, also 2RN, 'St Pantaleon in Prison'
S. Rocco, Church of, between 1 and 2LN, 'Christ driving out the Money-Changers'
S. Zaccaria

Gentile da Fabriano (c. 1360-1427)
See Chapter 2

Giambono, Michele (c. 1390-1462)
St Mark's, Capella della Madonna dei Mascoli (l.w.)
Acaddemia, Room I
Museo Correr, Room 6
S. Trovaso

Giorgione
See above

Guarana, Jacopo (1720-1808)
Palazzo Patriarcale, ceremonial hall ceiling
S. Benedetto, lunette above High Altar, 'St Benedict in Glory'
Cà Rezzonico, tapestry room ceiling
Scuola di S. Giovanni Evangelista, upper hall ceiling, 'Vision of Seven Angels', upper floor, archive room ceiling
S. Martino
S. Moisè
Ospedaletto, music room, frescoes
S. Pantaleone
Spirito Santo, R of High Altar, 'St Matthew'
S. Teresa, L of organ, 'Madonna and Saints'
S. Tomà
Grand Canal, frescoes, etc., in Palazzi Grassi, Michiel, Pisani-Moretta, Tron

Guardi, Francesco (1712-1793) and Gian Antonio (1699-1760)
Accademia, Room XVII
Angelo Raffaelle
Cà d'Oro, Room X
Cà Rezzonico, Rooms XIV, XVIII, XX
Museo Correr, Room VI

Guercino, Francesco Barbieri, called (1591-1666)
S. Lazzaro dei Mendicanti

Jacobello del Fiore (c. 1370-1439)
Doge's Palace, Sala Erizzo, 'Winged Lion'
Accademia, Room I
Museo Correr, Room 6

Licinio, Bernardino (1489-1550)
Accademia, Room VI, female portrait
Cà d'Oro, Room V' 'Portrait of a Young Woman'
Frari, ch. L of Ch., 'Madonna and Saints', and 'Franciscan Martyrs'.

Lippi, Filippino (1457-1504)
Ca d'Oro, Room IX, the 'Virgin in Adoration' (attribution doubtful)
Pinacoteca Manfrediana

Longhi, Alessandro, son of Pietro (1733-1813)
Accademia, Room XVI,
Cà d'Oro, Room VIII, portraits
Cà Rezzonico, Tiepolo Room, portrait
Museo Correr, Rooms VIII and IX, portraits
S. Pantaleone
Galleria Querini-Stampalia, Room XVIII, portrait

Longhi, Pietro (1702-1777)
Accademia, Rooms XVII and XVIII
Cà Rezzonico, Room XIX
Museo Correr, Room X
S. Pantaleone
Galleria Querini-Stampalia, Rooms XI, XII and XIII

Lorenzo Veneziano (c. 1325-1380)
Accademia, Room I
Museo Correr, Room 3

Lotto, Lorenzo (1480-1556)
Accademia, Room VII
Museo Correr, Room 17
S. Giacomo dell'Orio
SS. Giovanni e Paolo
S. Maria del Carmelo

Maffei, Francesco (1625-1660)
Accademia, Room XI, 'St Philip Neri'
SS. Apostoli
Cà Rezzonico, library ceiling
Galleria Querini-Stampalia, Room XIX

Mansueti, Giovanni (c. 1465-1527)
Accademia, Room XX, 'Interior', and Room XXIII, 'St Sebastian and other Saints'
S. Giovanni Crisostomo, flanking Bellini's 'St Jerome' and in chs. R and L of Ch. 'St John Chrysostom, St Onofrius, St Andrew and St Agatha'
Scuola di S. Marco, Sala dell' Albergo
S. Simeone Profeta, ch. L of Ch., 'Holy Trinity'
S. Martino on Burano (see Torcello and Burano)

Mantegna, Andrea (1431-1506)
St Mark's, Capella della Madonna dei Mascoli (r.w.)
Accademia, Room IV
Cà d'Oro, Room VI

Marconi, Rocco (c. 1480-1529)
Accademia, Rooms II and VIII, 'Woman taken in Adultery'
S. Cassiano
SS. Giovanni e Paolo
S. Trovaso, sacristy, 'Christ in Benediction'

Marieschi, Jacopo (1711-1794)
S. Francesco di Paola
S. Giovanni in Bragora, 2RN altar-piece 'St John the Almsgiver', and lunette L wall 'St John's Body brought to Venice'
S. Giovanni Elemosinario, sacristy ceiling, 'St John the Almsgiver'
S. Giovanni Evangelista, upper room ceiling, octagon farthest from altar and two adjoining pictures, all of 'St John'; Church, L wall and ceiling of Ch., 'The Last Supper' and 'Elevation of the Cross'
S. Maria del Giglio, RN and LN, 'Stations of the Cross', seventh and eighth
S. Maria dei Penitenti
S. Stefano, 3RN, the 'Immaculate Conception with St John Nepomuk and St Lucy'

Memling, Hans (1433-1494)
Accademia, Room IV

Messina, Antonello da (1430-1479)
See 'Antonello'

Montagna, Bartolomeo (1450-1523)
Accademia, Room XXIII,
Museo Correr, Room 14

Moretto da Brescia, Alessandro Bonvicino, called (1498-1554)
Accademia, Room VI, 'Madonna with Monks and Donors'
La Pietà

Negroponte, Antonio da (c. 1440-1490)
S. Francesco della Vigna

Palma, Giacomo, il Vecchio (1480-1528)
Accademia, Rooms III and VIII, also Room VI, 'St Peter and other Saints', Room VIII, 'Assumption'
S. Cassiano
Madonna dell'Orto, 2LN, 'St. Vincent and other Saints'
Scuola di S. Marco
S. Maria Formosa
Galleria Querini-Stampalia, Rooms VIII and IX, 'Holy Family'

Palma, Giacomo, il Giovane (1544-1628)
Doge's Palace:
    S.d. Senato, five pictures
    Ante-room of S.d. Maggior Consiglio, 'Doge and Saints before the Virgin with Allegories'
    S.d. Maggior Consiglio, 'Venice Crowned by Victory' and two adjacent pictures on ceiling, also 2L 'Andrea Gritti entering Padua'
    S.d. Scrutinio, 'Last Judgement'
Accademia, Room XIII
Angelo Raffaelle
S. Antonino
S. Bartolomeo
Cà d'Oro, Room VIII
S. Fantino
S. Francesco di Paola,
S. Francesco della Vigna, 3RN, 'Madonna in Glory', choir (l.w.), 'The Redeemer with Madonna and Saints'
Frari, Altar 4RN, 'Martyrdom of St Catherine', ch. on L of Ch. 'Pope Honorius and St Francis'
S. Geremia
Gesuiti, sacristy, ceiling and walls and 1RN, also Oratorio dei Crociferi
S. Giacomo dell'Orio, near sacristy, wall opposite entrance, small 'Crucifixion', ch. R of Ch., 'Road to Calvary' and 'Deposition', all in old sacristy, ch. of S. Lorenzo, 'St Lawrence' and 'Martyrdom of St Laurence'
S. Giorgio Maggiore, sacristy 'Presentation of Jesus'
S. Giorgio degli Schiavoni, e.w. 'St Francis'
S. Giovanni in Bragora, e.w. 'Christ before Caiaphas', Ch. 'Christ washing the Disciples' Feet'
S. Giovanni Elemosinario, LN, 'Constantine and the True Cross'
S. Giovanni Evangelista, albergo, side walls, four pictures

including 'Madonna Crowned with Stars' and 'Triumph of Death'

SS. Giovanni e Paolo, sacristy, 'Crucifixion and Saints' and 'Resurrection'

S. Lio

S. Luca

S. Maria Formosa

S. Maria del Giglio

S. Maria della Salute, sacristy, 'Jonah' and 'Samson'

S. Martino

Murano, Gli Angeli, RN, 'Madonna and Saints'

S. Nicolò dei Mendicoli

S. Nicolò da Tolentino, RT, altar-piece in ch., 'Virgin in Glory and Saints', 1 and 2 LN, walls and ceilings

Ospedaletto, 3RN, 'Annunciation'

S. Pantaleone, 2RN, 'Beheading of St Pantaleon'

S. Polo, High Altar, 'Conversion of St Paul' and four others in Ch.

Galleria Querini-Stampalia, Room IV, by window, 'Assumption'

Redentore, 1LN, 'Deposition'

S. Salvatore, 1LN, 'Virgin with St Antony and other Saints'

S. Sebastiano, ch. R of Ch., altar-piece, 'Virgin with St Jerome and St Charles'

S. Simeone Profeta, L. Wall 'Presentation'

Spirito Santo, 1LN, 'Marriage of the Virgin'

S. Trovaso, ch. in LT, altar-piece 'Deposition', 1LN, 'Birth of the Virgin', 2LN 'Virgin in Glory and Saints'

S. Zaccaria, 1RN, 'Virgin and Child with Saints'

S. Zulian, RN, ch. of S. Anastasio, 'David with the Head of Goliath'

Zitelle

Paolo Veneziano (1290-1362)

St Mark's, behind High Altar, 'Christ the Virgin and Saints' with 'Scenes from the Life of Christ and the Apostles' in the Museo Marciano

Accademia Room I

Museo Correr Room 2

Frari

Peranda, Sante (1566-1638)

Doge's Palace, S.d. Scrutinio, Piazzetta wall, L of second window from R, 'Naval Victory'

S. Bartolomeo

S. Fantino

Scuola di S. Giovanni Evangelista, upper hall 2R, 'St John boiled in Oil'

S. Nicolò da Tolentino, 1RN, 'Ecstasy of St Andrew', 3RN 'Adoration of the Magi', ch. in LT, 'St Gaetanus', 3LN various

S. Salvatore, LT, altar on L, 'Pietà with St Charles and Donors'

S. Stefano, sacristy, end wall, 'Martyrdom of St Stephen'

S. Zulian

Piazzetta, Giovanni Battista (1682-1754)

Accademia, Rooms XVIA and XVII

Cà Rezzonico

Gesuati

SS. Giovanni e Paolo

Scuola di S. Maria del Carmine

S. Maria della Fava

S. Salvatore, last LN, 'St Nicholas and the Blessed Archangelo Caneti' (finished by a pupil)

S. Stae

S. Vitale

Piero della Francesca (1416-1492)

Accademia, Room IV

Piombo, Sebastiano Luciani, called Sebastiano del (1485-1547)

Accademia, Room III

S. Bartolomeo

S. Giovanni Crisostomo

Pisanello, Antonio Pisano, called (c. 1390-1455)

Cà d'Oro, Room XV

Pitati, Bonifazio, of Verona, often called B. Veronese (1487-1553)

Accademia, Room VI, Room VIII, 'Slaughter of Innocents', also 'Annunciation', 'Christ and two Saints', 'God over St Mark's' Room IX 'Madonna and Saints'.

Cà d'Oro, Rooms VII and XI

S. Maria Mater Domini

S. Nicolo da Tolentino, 3RN, 'Beheading of St John the Baptist' and 'Herod's Feast'

Pittoni, Giovanni Battista (1687-1767)
Accademia, Corridor XV and Room XVII, 'Crassus sacking the Temple' and the 'Magdalen'
S. Cassiano, sacristy chapel, the 'Virgin and Child with St Charles Borromeo and St Philip Neri'
Frari
S. Giovanni Elemosinario
S. Stae

Ricci, Sebastiano (1659-1734)
Doge's Palace:
  Antichiesetta, cartoon for mosaic over second door from L of St Mark's
  S.d. Scrutinio, over two R windows on Piazzetta side, 'Two Allegorical Figures'
Accademia, Room XVII (but labelled 'Fontebasso')
Gesuati
S. Giorgio Maggiore
S. Maria del Carmelo
S. Marziale, ceiling of nave and chancel
S. Rocco, Church of
S. Stae
S. Vitale

Rubens, Peter Paul (1577-1640)
S. Maria del Giglio

Sante Peranda
See Peranda

Savoldo, Giovanni Gerolamo (1480-1550)
Accademia, Room VII
S. Giobbe

Schiavone, Andrea Meldolla, called (1522-1563)
Piazzetta, Libreria Sansoviniana
Accademia, Room XIII
S. Giacomo dell'Orio
S. Maria del Carmelo
Galleria Querini-Stampalia, Room V, 'Conversion of St Paul' (attribution uncertain)
S. Rocco, Church of
S. Sebastiano

Stefano da Zevio (1375-1450)
Museo Correr, Room 5

Strozzi, Bernardo (1581-1644)
Accademia, Rooms XI, 'Feast in the House of Simon', and XIV, 'Saints'
S. Benedetto
S. Nicolò da Tolentino
Galleria Querini-Stampalia, Room XIX
S. Zaccaria, RN above door, 'Tobias healing his Father'

Tiepolo, Giovanni Battista
See above

Tiepolo, Giovanni Domenico, son of G.B. (1727-1804)
Doge's Palace:
  S.d. Senato, L and R of Doge's Chair, 'Cicero denouncing Catiline' and 'Demosthenes addressing the People'
Accademia, Roomx XI and XVIII
Cà d'Oro, Room VIII
Cà Rezzonico
S. Francesco di Paola
Scuola di S. Giovanni Evangelista, upper hall, corner panels, 'Scenes from the Apocalypse'
S. Lio
S. Polo
S. Zaccaria, ch. of S. Anastasio, 'Flight into Egypt'

Tintoretto, Domenico, son of Jacopo (1560-1635)
Doge's Palace:
  Avogaria, S.d. Notai, L. of entrance 'St Mark with Sword and Scales'
  S.d. Censori, by entrance door, 'Annunciation with three Avogadori', also many on rest of frieze.
  Lobby of S.d. Maggior Consiglio, 'Doge Bembo before Venice'
  S.d. Maggior Consiglio, portraits of Doges, and on courtyard wall 'Battle of Salvore'
Cà d'Oro, Room XI

S. Fosca
S. Francesco della Vigna, Ch., 'Venice praying to the Virgin' (R. wall)
S. Giovanni Elemosinario, ch. R. of Ch., lunette of 'St

Catherine', R.e.w., lunette of 'God the Father with Donor and others'

Scuola di S. Giovanni Evangelista, upper hall, 1R, 'Fall of the Temple of Ephesus', 3R 'St John miraculously making a Dead Man speak', 4R 'Transfiguration', church RN 'Crucifixion'

The Madonna dell'Orto, after 1LN 'God the Father', 3LN 'Nativity' and two 'Angels'

Scuola di S. Marco

S. Marziale, outside Ch., 'Annunciation'

S. Trovaso, ch. R of Ch., 'Crucifixion'

Tintoretto, Jacopo
See above

Titian
See above

Tura, Cosimo (1430-1495)
Accademia, Room IV
Museo Correr, Room 7

Van Dyck, Antony (1599-1641)
Cà d'Oro, Room VII
S. Zaccaria

Veronese, Paolo
See above

Vivarini, Alvise, son of Antonio (1446-1505)
Accademia, Room XXIII
Museo Correr, Room 14
Frari
S. Giovanni in Bragora
SS. Giovanni e Paolo
Redentore

Vivarini, Antonio (1415-1480)
Accademia, Rooms I and XXIV, 'Madonna' in triptych
Cà d'Oro, Room I, polyptych (attribution uncertain)
S. Francesco della Vigna, e.w., 'St Jerome', 'St Bernard', and 'St Louis' (attribution uncertain)
S. Giobbe
S. Pantaleone
S. Zaccaria

Vivarini, Bartolomeo, brother of Antonio (1432-1500)
Accademia, Room XXIII
Museo Correr, Room 8
S. Eufemia
Frari
S. Giovanni in Bragora
SS. Giovanni e Paolo, 1LN, 'St Augustine', 'St Dominic' and 'St Laurence'
S. Maria Formosa
S. Stefano
Also, in the glass museum at Murano,. glass museum, the 'Madonna'

Zanchi, Antonio (1631-1722)
S. Canciano
Pinacoteca Manfrediana
Scuola di S. Maria del Carmine, main upper room, between windows facing entrance 'Miraculous Cures of the Virgin'
S. Maria del Giglio
S. Marziale, 1RN 'The Redeemer and Three Saints'
Murano, S. Michele in Isola, e.w., 'Plague of Serpents'
Galleria Querini-Stampalia, Room VI, e.w. top L 'St Jerome'
Scuola di S. Rocco, stairway, upper flight R, the 'Virgin appearing to the Plague-Stricken'
S. Zaccaria, over 1RN, e.w. 'St Zacharias in the Temple', over sacristy door, LN 'Procession of Bodies of Saints'
S. Zulian

Zuccarelli, Frencesco (1702–1778)
Accademia, Corridor XII
Cà Rezzonico, hall on second floor 'Pastoral Scene', Room XXI 'Landscape'

ARCHITECTS AND SCULPTORS

Abbondi
See Scarpagnino

Aspetti, Tiziano (1565-1607)
Piazzetta, statues flanking door of Biblioteca Marciana (with Campagna)
Doge's Palace: Scala d'Oro, statues flanking entrance, Ante-

Collegio, statues, etc., on window wall round and over fireplace, Armoury rooms

S. Francesco della Vigna, facade, statues of 'Moses' and 'St Paul', Cappella dei Grimani, 5LN, 'Justice' and 'Temperance'

Grand Canal, reliefs of 'St Mark' and 'St Theodore' on Rialto bridge

Bon, Bartolomeo, of Bergamo (c. 1440-1529)

Piazza S. Marco, Campanile, main design and supervision of original

Scuola di S. Rocco

Bon, Bartolomeo, son of Giovanni (c. 1395-1465)

St Mark's, Cappella di S. Maria dei Mascoli, the 'Virgin and Child with St Mark and St John'

Doge's Palace, Porta della Carta and Foscari Porch

Cà d'Oro

The Misericordia

Scuola di S. Marco

Also S. Carità, now part of the Accademia

Bon, Giovanni (c. 1360-1440)

Associated with his son Bartolomeo in Doge's Palace, Porta della Carta and Loggia, and Cà d'Oro

Bregno, Antonio and Paolo, brothers, of Como (mid 15th century)

Doge's Palace:
    corner nearest St Mark's, above, 'Archangel Gabriel'
    Porta della Carta, above, 'Prudence' and 'Charity' (attribution uncertain); entrance to courtyard and arch at end of entrance, part of decoration

Frari, Ch. R wall, monument to Doge Francesco Foscari

Bregno, Lorenzo (c. 1460-1523)

St Mark's, chancel

Frari

S. Giobbe

S. Maria Mater Domini

Campagna, Girolamo (1550-1630)

Piazzetta, statues flanking door of Biblioteca Marciana (with Aspetti)

Doge's Palace, S.d. Quattro Porte, door to Senato, 'Athene' between 'War' and 'Peace'

Frari

Gesuiti

S. Giacomo di Rialto

S. Giorgio Maggiore

SS. Giovanni e Paolo, Ch. further monument on R, statue of 'Doge Loredan', Cappella del Rosario, on balustrade of High Altar, 'St Thomas Aquinas' and 'St Rose' (ruined)

S. Giuseppe di Castello

S. Maria del Carmelo

S. Maria Formosa, ch. R of Ch., 'St Francis', 'St Laurence' and 'St Sebastian' (attribution not quite certain)

S. Maria dei Miracoli

Redentore

Scuola di S. Rocco

S. Sebastiano

S. Stefano

S. Tomà

S. Zulian

Canova, Antonio (1759-1822)

Accademia, Corridor XVIII

Museo Correr

Pinacoteca Manfrediana

Galleria Querini-Stampalia, Room VII

Also Naval Museum, 2nd Floor, main room, against wall opposite entrance, monument to Admiral Emo

Coducci, Mauro (1440-1504)

Piazza S. Marco, Procuratie Vecchie and Clock-Tower

S. Giovanni Crisostomo

Scuola di S. Giovanni Evangelista

Scuola di S. Marco

S. Maria Formosa

Murano, S. Michele in Isola

S. Pietro di Castello

S. Zaccaria

Grand Canal, P. Corner-Spinelli (No. 12), P. Vendramin Calergi (No. 18)

Donatello (1382-1466)

Frari

Francesco di Giorgio (1451-1502)
S. Maria del Carmelo

Gambello, Antonio (1430-1481)
Arsenale
San Giobbe
SS. Giovanni e Paolo
S. Zaccaria

Grigi, Guglielmo dei (c. 1475-1530)
Piazza S. Marco Procuratie Vecchie
SS. Giovanni e Paolo
Murano, S. Michele in Isola
S. Salvatore
Grand Canal, P. dei Camerlenghi (No. 15)

Lamberti, Nicolò (c. 1380-1456), and his son Pietro (c. 1400-1465)
St Mark's, exterior
Doge's Palace, exterior
SS. Giovanni e Paolo
Scuola di S. Marco

Leopardi, Alessandro (1460-1522)
Piazza S. Marco
SS. Giovanni e Paolo (outside), Colleoni statue
S. Stefano

Lombardo, the Solari family, called: Pietro (1435-1515) and his sons, Tullio (1460-1532) and Antonio (1463-1516)
St Mark's, Zen Chapel, Antonio
Doge's Palace, courtyard decoration, Pietro
SS. Apostoli, Tullio
Cà d'Oro, Room III, Tullio
S. Francesco della Vigna, ch. L of Ch., 'Prophets', Pietro, 'Evangelists' Tullio and Antonio
Frari, choir, Pietro
S. Giobbe, Pietro
S. Giovanni Crisostomo, Tullio
S. Giovanni Evangelista, Pietro
SS. Giovanni e Paolo, Pietro and Tullio
S. Lio, Pietro and Tullio
Pinacoteca Manfrediana, Pietro
Scuola di S. Marco, all three
S. Maria dei Miracoli, all three

S. Martino, Tullio
S. Maria della Salute, ante-sacristy, relief of 'Pietà and Saints', Tullio
S. Salvatore, Tullio
S. Stefano, sacristy, over door to smaller sacristy, head of 'Young Man', Tullio, 3LN 'St Paul' and 'St Jerome', Pietro
Grand Canal, P. Dario (No. 2), Pietro
Also Scuola dei Calegheri, in Campo S. Tomà, figure of 'St Mark' on facade, Pietro

Longhena, Baldassare (1598-1682)
S. Antonino
Cà Rezzonico
Frari
Scuola di S. Maria del Carmine
S. Maria della Salute (and Seminario Patriarcale adjoining)
S. Nicolo da Tolentino
S. Pietro di Castello
Gli Scalzi
Grand Canal, P. Pesaro (No. 17), P. Giustinian-Lolin, P. Belloni-Battaggia
Also Scuola di S. Nicolo, adjoining S. Giorgio dei Greci

Martini, Francesco di Giorgio (1455-1502)
See Francesco

Masegne, Jacobello and Pietro-Paolo delle (late 14th century)
St Mark's:
    Façade, decorative work
    Iconostasis 'Virgin, St Mark and Twelve Apostles'
    ch. on R. of Ch. and ch. on L. of Ch.
Doge's Palace, Molo facade, central balcony and windows
Museo Correr, Room 4
SS. Giovanni e Paolo, ch. 2L of Ch.

Nino Pisano (c. 1320-1370)
SS. Giovanni e Paolo, Ch.

Accademia Palladio, Andrea (1508-1580)
Doge's Palace, decoration of Collegio and Ante-Collegio (part), doors of S.d. Quattro Porte (part)
S. Francesco della Vigna
S. Giorgio Maggiore (and refectory and cloisters of adjoining Convent)
Redentore

Riccio, Andrea Briosco, called (1470-1532)
Cà d'Oro, Rooms I, XI and XIII
Museo Correr, Room 17

Rizzo, Antonio (1440-1500)
Doge's Palace
S. Elena
Frari
S. Luca
Murano, S. Maria d. Angeli, bas-relief over entrance (but attribution very doubtful)

Robbia, della
S. Giobbe

Roccatagliata, Nicolò and Sebastiano (son of Nicolò) (c. 1565-1640)
S. Giorgio Maggiore
S. Moisè

Sanctis, Giovanni de (c. 1330-1392)
St Mark's

Sanmicheli, Michele (1484-1559)
P. Corner-Mocenigo, S. Polo
Grand Canal, P. Grimani (No. 13) and P. Gussoni-Grimani della Vida (near Cà d'Oro)
Also arch near Ponte S. Giuseppe and fort of S. Andrea, Lido

Sansovino, Jacopo Tatti, called (1486-1570)
Piazza S. Marco and Piazzetta, Loggetta and Libreria Sansoviniana
St Mark's
Doge's Palace
S. Fantino
S. Francesco della Vigna
Frari
Scuola di S. Marco (part)
S. Martino
S. Salvatore, also cloisters (attributed)
S. Sebastiano
S. Zulian
Grand Canal, P. Corner (No. 1), P. Manin Dolfin, now Banca d'Italia on R. just before Rialto Bridge, Fabbriche Nuove or Erberia, arcades on L just beyond Rialto Bridge
Also P. Priuli-Stazio, near S. Stae

Sardi, Giuseppe (c. 1635-1699)
S. Lazzaro dei Mendicanti, including design for facade
Madonna dell'Orto, beyond 3RN, monument to G. Cavazza
S. Maria del Giglio
Ospedaletto
S. Pantaleone
S. Salvatore, facade
Gli Scalzi
Grand Canal, P. Michiel dalle Colonne, 4th before Cà d'Oro, P. Flangini, next beyond S. Geremia
Also P. Savorgnan, near S. Geremia, Scuola di S. Teodoro, opposite S. Salvatore, now a cinema

Scamozzi, Vincenzo (1552-1616)
Piazza S. Marco, Procuratie Nuove
Piazzetta, Libreria Sansoviniana, completion after Sansovino's death, including main door
SS. Giovanni e Paolo, sacristy door
S. Nicolò da Tolentino
Grand Canal, P. Contarini degli Scrigni

Scarpagnino, Antonio delli Abbondi, called (c. 1475-1549)
S. Fantino
S. Giovanni Elemosinario
Scuola di S. Rocco
S. Sebastiano
Grand Canal, Fondaco dei Tedeschi (No. 15) (with Spavento), P. Contarini delle Figure, Fabbriche Vecchie
Also P. dei dieci Savi, W. end of Rialto Bridge opposite P. dei Camerlenghi, P. Loredan in Campo Morosini

Spavento, Giorgio (c. 1440-1509)
Piazza S. Marco, initial design of Campanile
Doge's Palace, reconstruction of N side (part)
S. Salvatore, first plan and Ch.
Grand Canal, Fondaco dei Tedeschi (with Scarpagnino)

Torretti, Giuseppe (1660-1743)
Gesuiti
S. Maria Formosa, altar front and frame of Palma Vecchio's 'St Barbara'
S. Stae, exterior decoration (part), 1LN, Crucifix and monuments

Verrocchio, Andrea (1436-1488)
SS. Giovanni e Paolo, outside, Colleoni statue

Vittoria, Alessandro (1524-1608)

Doge's Palace:
  Scala d'Oro, stucco decoration
  S.d. Quattro Porte, door to Ante-Collegio, 'Vigilance' between 'Eloquence' and 'Fluency'
  Ante-Collegio, door to Collegio, 'Venice between 'Concord' and 'Glory'
  At exit of armoury rooms
S. Antonino
Cà d'Oro, hall on 1st floor and Rooms III and VII
Cà Rezzonico, hall on 1st floor
Museo Correr, Room XIII
S. Francesco della Vigna
Frari
S. Giacomo di Rialto
S. Giorgio Maggiore
SS. Giovanni e Paolo, last LN, Cap. del Rosario, and LN, over sacristy door, bust of Titian (ascription doubtful)
S. Giuseppe di Castello
Madonna dell'Orto
Pinacoteca Manfrediana
S. Maria del Giglio, 2RN, inside oratory door, bust of Girolamo Molin, L wall of chancel, bust of Giulio Contarini

S. Maria dei Miracoli
Murano, S. Maria degli Angeli
S. Polo
S. Salvatore
S. Sebastiano
S. Stefano
S. Zaccaria
S. Zulian
Grand Canal, P. Grimani (No. 13)

Some artists mentioned in the text are not included above because their works in Venice are scanty or uneven or both, however well they may be presented elsewhere. The best known of these are Federico Bencovich (1670-c. 1745); Rosalba Carriera (1675-1757); Gian Antonio Pellegrini (1675-1741); Pordenone, *viz* G. A. Sacchiense (1484-1539); Andrea Previtali (c. 1475-1528); and Angelo Trevisani (1669-1758).